> "We are rough men used to rough ways."
> —BOB YOUNGER, AMERICAN OUTLAW

First Edition • October, 1999

Published by Tri Star - Boze Publications, Inc. • 3110 North 35th Avenue, Suite 4 • Phoenix, Arizona 85017
602-269-2900 • 800-350-6345 • Facsimile 602-269-1469
ISBN 1-887576-06-1 (Soft Cover) • ISBN 1-887576-07-X (Hardbound)

BAD MEN

OUTLAWS &
GUNFIGHTERS
of the
WILD WEST

WRITTEN AND
ILLUSTRATED BY
BOB BOZE BELL

Killing Me Softly With Her Logic

Several years ago, while vacationing in San Francisco, my wife and I were in a bookstore and she pointed out to me a slate of mug shots from the 1880s. They were for sale, and much to my wife's surprise I took one look and said I wasn't interested. Her incredulous expression at my answer caused me to question my disinterest: after all, here were multiple photos of Old West Bad Men, actually carried in the saddlebags of a northern California sheriff! What was my problem?

In a nutshell: the mugshots were of San Francisco Bad Men—to me they were not outlaws, but urban criminals.

This led to the following question from my wife: "Do you mean to say that if these same thugs were wearing hats with wider brims, and committing the same crimes, but on horseback, outside the city limits—way out on the desert, they would somehow, be magically transformed into courageous, awe-inspiring outlaws?"

"Right as rain, Ms. Ryder."

"Bob, you are one crazy wacko!"

"Not you sir," I told the owner, whose name is also Bob. "My wife is referring to me."

"You're all wacko!" she barked as she shook her head in disgust and left the store. "All of you Old West Nuts are certifiably crazy!"

Somewhat embarrassed, I turned to face my fellow book buyers: "Actually, she should know," I told them matter-of-factly, "my wife is a therapist."

I didn't admit it that balmy day in the musty stacks of the Argonaut Bookstore, but my therapist wife is right. I really can't defend my interest, nay—my passion—for Old West Bad Men. I can't even rationalize it. Perhaps you will allow me to try and illustrate it. (BBB)

February 20, 1999
Bob Boze Bell
Cave Creek, Arizona

HERE'S WHAT I WANTED THEM TO LOOK LIKE!

JAMES BECKWOURTH

A mulatto mountain of a man who was a free trapper in the 1820s. In his almost 40 years on the frontier, he stole horses, fought Indians, joined the Crow tribe, married several of their women, joined war parties, guided military expeditions, wintered in Florida and fought in the Seminole War (1837), helped put down an insurrection (Taos, 1847), joined the gold rush and dictated his memoirs (which everyone agrees is loaded up with tall tales). He died in 1866 among the Crow tribe and was buried as a warrior on a tree platform. (Bob McCubbin Collection)

1836

February 25, 1836
Samual Colt receives a patent for his new revolver, the Colt .45.

March 6, 1836
The Alamo falls.

1837

The Texas Rangers are organized.

May 27, 1837
Polly Butler Hickok gives birth to her fourth son, James Butler Hickok, in Homer, Illinois.

June 20, 1837
Queen Victoria succeeds to the British throne at age 18.

1840

*The saxophone is invented in Belgium.
The Rocky Mountain fur trade comes to an end.*

December 28, 1841
The Rev. Robert James marries Zerelda Cole in Stamping Ground, Kentucky.

November 4, 1842
Mary Todd, 23, marries Abraham Lincoln, 33, in Springfield, Illinois.

1846

*The Donner Party is trapped in the snows near Truckee, California.
Elias Howe's sewing machine is patented.
Oregon is acquired from Great Britain and becomes a state.
Texas' war with Mexico for independence begins.*

January 3, 1846
The term "Manifest Destiny" is used for the very first time in Congress by Robert Winthrop of Massachusetts.

September 30, 1846

Dr. William Morton, a dentist in Massachusetts, extracts a tooth with the help of anesthesia. It is a first.

1847

Jim Bridger leads 15,000 Mormons across the Rocky Mountains to the shores of Great Salt Lake.

September 5, 1847

Jesse Woodson James is born in Clay County, Missouri.

January 24, 1848

While inspecting the debris from a millrace construction site on the American River in California, foreman, James Marshall, picks up a small nugget of gold. The rush begins.

December 5, 1848

A bandit gang of failed gold seekers and Naval deserters rob and kill ten men, women and children at Mission San Miguel, California.

January, 1849

At Dry Diggings, California, three robbers are tried by a miner's court and hanged. This is the first lynching in the region and the camp becomes known as Hangtown [later, Placerville].

1850

Allan Pinkerton starts a detective agency in Chicago, Illinois.

June-July, 1851

The San Francisco Committee of Vigilance hangs four men.

August 14, 1851

John Henry Holliday is born in Griffin, Georgia.

February 24, 1852

Roy Bean fights a duel at San Diego, California, wounding his opponent. Both participants are thrown in jail [Bean escapes on March 6 and heads for Los Angeles, where he soon fights another duel].

ROUGH ETHICS FOR A ROUGH TOWN

All whipsawed wood and haphazard angles, Hangtown, California, was as rough as they come. It was here Jesse James' father died. He wasn't alone. In 1855, there were 47 lynchings and nine legal hangings in the state of California. (CALIFORNIA STATE LIBRARY, SACRAMENTO)

CULTURE CLASH

It didn't take long for the newly landed 49ers (at left) to get crossways with the Spanish caballeros (at right) who had been dominant in the California region for most of two centuries. Bad Men of both persuasions fanned the flames of distrust and hatred.

(BBB)

SAN DIEGO OLD TOWN

It was here, in the scraggly, small port town of San Diego, that Roy Bean fought an illegal duel in 1852. He was jailed but escaped to another small, but wild town, Los Angeles. (RUDOLPH SCHILLER PHOTO, 1869)

DEATH TO JOAQUIN MURRIETA!

CAPTAIN LOVE
(WELLS FARGO BANK)

(AC)

Joaquin Murrieta
(BBB)

California Ranger Harry Love (above, left) and his men captured Joaquin's brother-in-law, Jesus Feliz, and forced him to guide the rangers to Murrieta's camp on Cantua Creek. Four of the outlaws were slain, including Bernadino Garcia, alias Three-Fingered Jack (AKA Four-Fingered Jack). Murrieta's head was cut off (as was Garcia's hand) and packed in whiskey until the posse could reach Sacramento, and claim the $1,000 reward. Love exhibited Joaquin's head for $1 a view (see poster above, left) in the central California mining camps where Murrieta was well-known. Eventually the "trophy" was acquired by Dr. Louis Jordan's San Francisco museum where it spent 30 years before being destroyed in the 1906 San Francisco earthquake. From the very beginning there were those who refused to believe Murrieta was actually killed (as is the case with so many outlaws). In the 1950s and 60s this refrain gained credence when several authors maintained there never was a Joaquin Murrieta, and that Ranger Love faked the entire jar episode, using some poor Indian's cabeza as a float-in. However, research by California authors, William Secrest and John Boessenecker, has convincingly proven there is simply too much contemporary evidence and too many eye witnesses who knew Joaquin in the mining camps and who testified it was, in fact, the infamous bandido in the jar.

July 13, 1852
Wells Fargo Express opens its California office in San Francisco.

September 13-14, 1852
Bandit Chieftain Claudio Feliz, brother-in-law of Joaquin Murrieta, and two of his band are killed resisting arrest near Monterey, California.

July, 1853
The California legislature lists five outlaw "Joaquins" as wanted: Joaquin Murrieta, Joaquin Valenzuela, Joaquin Carillo, Joaquin Botellier and Joaquin Ocomorenia.

July 25, 1853
California Rangers with Captain Harry Love kill the infamous bandido, Joaquin Murrieta and Three-Fingered Jack.

1854
The Kansas-Nebraska Act opens lands to settlers previously reserved by treaty for the Indians.

February 28, 1854
The U.S. Republican Party is officially formed.

November 15, 1855
Surrounded by a sheriff's posse near Monterey, California, bandit leader Anastacio Garcia kills two possemen and wounds three before escaping.

February 14, 1856
Renowned bandido, Felipe Carabajal, is cornered by a posse under a bridge near Oakland, California. Felipe manages to wound one posse member before he is shot dead.

May-September, 1856
The Committee of Vigilance in San Francisco hangs four men and deports 40 more to Hawaii and South America.

August 11, 1856

The Tom Bell gang attempts to rob a stagecoach near Marysville, California. In a shootout that ensues, Mrs. Tilghman and another passenger are killed.

1857

A yellow fever epidemic rips through New Orleans taking 7,000 lives.

January 27, 1857

Los Angeles Sheriff James Barton and three of his posse are ambushed and murdered by the Juan Flores-Pancho Daniel gang.

[A huge manhunt ensues: two suspected gang members are shot dead, 11 are lynched and one legally hung.]

February 16, 1857

Under indictment for six murders, Anastacio Garcia is lynched in the Monterey jail.

The Monterey Jail (AC)

March 6, 1857

The Supreme Court hands down the Dred Scott Decision which declares that a slave is not a citizen and therefore cannot sue for his freedom in a federal court. Chief Justice Taney states that the constitution was made by and for white men.

August 26, 1857

Tiburcio Vasquez is imprisoned at San Quentin (he will escape on June 25, 1859).

September 11, 1857

In Utah, Mormons led by John D. Lee attack a wagon train, killing 100 men, women and children.

"[In Mexico and Old California] the line of demarcation between rebel and robber, pillager and patriot was dimly defined."
—HORACE BELL, LOS ANGELES RANGER

(BOB MCCUBBIN COLLECTION)

TIBURCIO VASQUEZ DEFENDS HIS CAREER CHOICE

"My career grew out of the circumstances by which I was surrounded. As I grew to manhood I was in the habit of attending balls and parties given by the native Californians, into which the Americans, then beginning to become numerous, would force themselves and shove the native born men aside, monopolizing the dance and the women. This was about 1852. I had numerous fights in defense of what I believed to be my rights and those of my countrymen...I believed we were unjustly and wrongly deprived of the social rights that belonged to us...I went to my mother and told her I intended to commence a different life. I asked for her blessing, and at once commenced the career of a robber."

—Tiburcio Vasquez   (BBB)

(BBB)

1858

*The Mason Jar is invented.
Minnesota becomes the
32nd state.*

May 12, 1858

The Jack Powers-Pio Linares bandit gang attacks Rancho San Juan Capistrano and kills two men, loots the ranch, kidnaps the foreman's wife, Andrea Baratie, and rapes her.

[A vigilance committee is formed and quickly tracks down the gang, lynching seven, killing Pio Linares and driving Jack Powers into Mexico.]

July 8, 1859

In Tubac, Arizona, Sylvester Mowry and newspaper editor, Edward Cross, fight a duel with Burnside rifles at 40 paces. Cross took issue with Mowry's claims of the territory's population. According to witnesses: "No blood flowed."

August 17, 1859

Tiburcio Vasquez is back in prison after the June 25th escape.

August 28, 1859

Oil is discovered at Titusville, Pennsylvania and launches a new era of lighting by kerosene.

September 28, 1859

The Juan Cortina gang (or, "brigade," depending on your point of view) invades Brownsville, Texas and kills four citizens. [Two days later a posse chases the bandits and captures Thomas Cabrera. Cortina demands his release or he will burn down the town. Cabrera is hanged on November tenth. On the 22nd, Tobin's Rangers set out to capture Cortina, get into a running gunfight with the outlaws and retreat to Brownsville.]

November 23, 1859

The birthday given of Henry McCarty [Billy the Kid].

JUAN NEPOMUCENO CORTINA

A rancher, general, governor, bandit and revolutionary, "Cheno" Cortina was a member of a wealthy and prominent family around the Brownsville, Texas area. A natural born leader, he fought constantly against what he saw as Mexicans being pushed into a state of second-class citizenship. In 1859 he became a hero to his people when he shot a Brownsville marshal over the beating of a former employee of Cortina's. Attempts by the Texas Rangers to arrest him were unsuccessful. He continued his resistance (see Sept. 28, 1859) and finally fled to Mexico where he was appointed a general (and later governor) by President Benito Juarez. After Porfirio Diaz came to power, Cortina was imprisoned in Mexico City for 17 years, being released in 1890. He returned to the border area and died in 1892. (BOB MCCUBBIN COLLECTION)

CALIFORNIO BANDIDO SLANG

All terms taken from newspapers and documents from the 1860s and 1870s.

- **Valentonado**—a boaster
- **Tapadera**—a fence; someone who fences stolen goods
- **"¡Pendejo!"**—an oath: Imbecile! or worse
- **"¡Bustante, senior!"**—That's enough, sir!
- **"¡No tiras!"**—Don't shoot!
- **mescarte**—hair rope
- **conocidos**—suspects
- **"leg bail"**—running away from an officer of the law
- to **"peach"**—rat out a comrade, as in, "The sheriff got one of his compadres to peach on him."
- **"go down into his boots"**—to shrink from fear, or humiliation, as in, "Soto challenged Procopio to fight and made him go down into his boots."
- **"too thin"**—a transparent lie, as in, "That's too thin, I know what you're up to."
- **"a sell"**—false information, as in, "That Tapadera gave you a sell."
- **"git up and dust"**—to ride quickly away from danger, as in, "If you see the sheriff's posse, git up and dust."
- **jackassable**—not navigable, even on a jackass, as in, "That road isn't passable, not even jackassable."

"It is my unbiased opinion that California can and does furnish the best bad things that are obtainable in America."
—HINTON HELPER, 1855

ALL ILLUSTRATIONS, (BBB)

Mickey Free:
Kidnapped and raised by Apaches, a friend says he is "part-Irish, part-Apache and all Son-of-a-Bitch."

Description:
"Of disreputable appearance," light complected with long reddish-blond hair and grey eyes (left eye gouged out by an elk horn in a childhood hunting accident).

Rank:
First sergeant of the Apache Scouts under Al Sieber. Can speak Spanish, English and Apache, however, is a so-so interpreter (Geronimo refuses to negotiate with Free as the interpreter, accusing him of twisting his words).

MICKEY FREE (AC)

1860

The Pony Express begins. Abraham Lincoln is elected president. The internal combustion engine is patented in Paris.

January 21, 1861

A prominent rancher's son is kidnapped by Apaches near Sonoita, Arizona, setting off a 20-year war with Cochise. [The boy grows up as an Apache and is given the name Mickey Free. See photo at left.]

April 26, 1861

Near Las Vegas, New Mexico, Paula Angel is hanged for the murder of Juan Martin. [Angel becomes the first woman to be hanged in New Mexico.]

July 7, 1861

Longhair Sam Brown, who boasts of killing 11 men and coining the phrase, "I want a man for supper," is killed near Genoa, Nevada Territory.

July 12, 1861

Wild Bill Hickok shoots it out with the McCanles crowd at Rock Creek Station, Nebraska.

April 16, 1862

The Confederate Congress orders all white men between the ages of 18 and 35 to be conscripted in the armed forces of the South.

July 6, 1862

In Virginia City, Nevada, journalist Samuel Langhorn Clemens begins using the pen name Mark Twain.

November 6, 1862

Instant communication between San Francisco and New York is instituted today with the completion of the transcontinental telegraph line.

VIRGINIA CITY, NEVADA
The second big boomtown of the West. It was here that Mark Twain was robbed by suspiciously familiar outlaws. (CARELTON WATKINS PHOTO, AC)

November 17, 1862

Prominent Los Angeles County rancher John Rains, owner of the Rancho Cucamonga, is lassoed from his wagon, dragged through cactus and shot to death. Suspects include vaqueros Procopio Bustamente, Manuel Cerrada and Tal Juanito. [Cerrada is later captured, confesses and claims that Don Ramon Carrillo, a prominent ranchero and enemy of Rains, paid them $500 to do the killing. Tal Juanito is shot to death in April of 1863, but Procopio escapes and makes his way back north, to his home range, the Alisal.]

1863

Quantrill's Raiders sack and burn Lawrence, Kansas.
The Battle of Gettysburg is fought.
Perrier water is introduced in France.

August 13, 1863

Tiburcio Vasquez is released from San Quentin prison.

September 4, 1863

After shooting a deputy, Procopio Bustamente is captured and sent to the state prison for nine years.

October 3, 1863

President Abraham Lincoln issues a proclamation making Thanksgiving a national holiday to be observed annually on the last Thursday in November.

January 10, 1864

In Montana, the Vigilante Committee hangs outlaw Sheriff Henry Plummer on a gallows built by the lawman himself. The pleading, crying Plummer and two confederates are lifted onto the shoulders of the vigilantes and then tossed into the air to strangle to death.

RAIDIN', RIDIN' & 'RITHMATIC

Quantrill's Raiders spawned an entire class of outlaws that will create havoc in the border states after the Civil War. Amazingly, some did become respectable citizens and there was even a lawmen or two, but not those pictured above. (BBB)

HANG 'EM HIGH, HANG 'EM LOW, JUST HANG 'EM!

Frontier hangings seemed to go in spurts. Locals would tolerate lawlessness to a certain point then they would start hanging any Bad Men they could find, until it became almost an epidemic. (ABOVE LEFT PHOTO, BUFFALO BILL HISTORICAL SOCIETY; ABOVE RIGHT PHOTO, COLORADO HISTORICAL SOCIETY)

Vigilante Tradition

Montana vigilantes traditionally buried lynched Bad Men in graves 3 feet wide, 7 feet deep and 77 inches long. To this day, the badges of the Montana Highway Patrol bear the vigilante symbol: "3-7-77."

JACK SLADE

Son of a U.S. marshal and Congressman from Illinois, Slade killed a man and fled to the West. He became a wagon boss and stage driver on the Overland Trail. He later "sanitized" the roughest section of the Overland Trail, by hanging and executing numerous stage robbers, crooked ranchers and horse thieves. After decamping to Virginia City, Montana, and because of his drinking and rowdyism, Slade himself was marked for execution by the infamous Vigilante Executive Committee of Montana (see March 10, 1864). (BBB)

January 14, 1864
At Virginia City, Montana, vigilantes hang another five men: Club Foot George Lane, Jack Gallagher, Frank Parrish, Haze Lyon and Boone Helm. A sixth man, Bill Hunter, escapes [but is recaptured and hung on Feb. 1].

January 21, 1864
At a place called Hell Gate, Montana, vigilantes hang eight men.

February 9, 1864
Vigilantes in Aurora, Nevada hang four men suspected of murder.

March 4, 1864
Three men are hanged by vigilantes in Lewiston, Idaho.

March 10, 1864
The infamous Jack Slade is hanged by vigilantes at Virginia City, Montana (see sidebar).

June 30, 1864
Riding as "Partisan Rangers," a group of San Jose, California area guerrillas, led by Missouri Bushwhacker, Captain Henry Ingram, stop and rob a Virginia City coach carrying $26,000 in bullion and coin. Capt. Ingram leaves a receipt certifying that the captured plunder will be used to "outfit recruits in California for the Confederate States Army."

July 6, 1864
Two Partisan Rangers, Jim Grant and Washington Jordan, stop a Los Angeles bound stage 22 miles south of San Juan Bautista, relieving passengers of $60.

July 9, 1864
Not satisfied with the earlier haul, Grant and Jordan stop the northbound stage at the same spot, but get even less.

July 16, 1864
While waiting at a ranch to attack a payroll coach, Captain Ingram and his main unit of

Partisan Rangers are attacked by a posse led by Santa Clara County Sheriff John Adams. With barking pistols and shotguns, three of the five Confederate guerrillas are shot to pieces, but Ingram and another rebel escape.

August 5, 1864

Confederate guerrillas, Jim Grant and Washington Jordan, halt the Visalia stage near Pacheco Pass and get $113 from the passengers.

August 8, 1864

Grant is captured by lawmen at a farm while visiting his girlfriend. Attempting to escape, Grant receives two barrels of shotgun pellets in the lower back, but, incredibly, he survives.

August 10, 1864

A vigilante committee in Dayton, Nevada, binds and gags the sheriff, takes a suspected killer out of jail and hangs him in the yard.

September 27, 1864

At Centralia, Missouri, Bloody Bill Anderson leads a Quantrill band on a raid, killing 25 unarmed Union soldiers. On leaving the area the guerrillas are pursued by Union troops. Anderson sets an ambush and 100 soldiers are killed including their leader, Major A.V.E. Johnson. Jesse James is often credited with the killing of Johnson.

1865

The Civil War ends. Lincoln is assassinated. The 13th Amendment abolishes slavery.

May 5, 1865

The first civilian train holdup in the United States comes off at North Bend, Ohio, when bandits derail the train. The outlaws loot the express car and rob the male passengers.

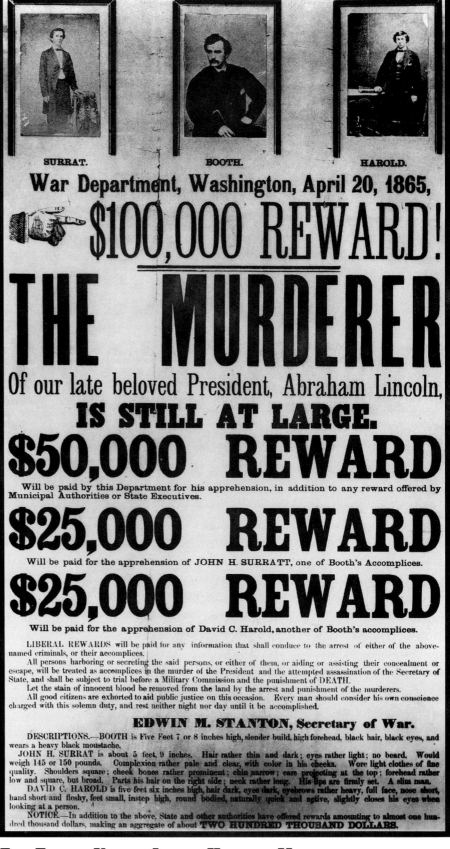

THE ENTIRE NATION IS IN A HANGING MOOD

No expense was spared for the capture and execution of those responsible for the murder of "our late beloved President, Abraham Lincoln." Of the prime suspects, Booth was shot and killed, and four others, including a woman, were hung. (AC)

THE SALT LAKE CITY STAGE, 1869 (CHARLES CARTER PHOTO, AC)

BUSHWHACKERS LOOKING FOR A NEW LINE OF WORK
(left to right): *Fletcher Taylor, Frank James and Jesse James, 1864.*
(MISSOURI STATE HISTORICAL SOCIETY)

May 10, 1865

Guerrilla leader Quantrill is killed by Union soldiers 30 miles southeast of Louisville, Kentucky. He was only 27 years old at the time of his death.

June 29, 1865

Three men hold up a stagecoach near Silver City, Nevada and get $14,000 from the Wells Fargo Express. [All three men are caught within three days and jailed in Dayton.]

July 10, 1865

The first rails of the Union Pacific Railroad are laid in Omaha, Nebraska. [These tracks will eventually join the Union Pacific at Promontory Point, Utah on May 10, 1869.]

July 13, 1865

A stagecoach from Salt Lake City bound for Montana is robbed by the remaining members of the notorious Plummer gang. A passenger named Parker fires on the bandits and shots are exchanged. Two women and two men in the coach are killed. Parker is wounded. The bandits get about $120,000 in gold dust. Frank Williams, the driver, runs into the brush and escapes injury. [Many begin to suspect that he was involved, but no proof is found. Years later, his body is found hanging from a tree near Denver, Colorado. His death is never explained.]

July 18, 1865

Noted gunfighter, pugilist and politician of the gold rush area, Billy Mulligan, shoots it out with San Francisco policemen. Three men die, including Mulligan.

(BBB)

July 21, 1865

Two hot-headed young men fight a street duel in Springfield, Missouri. They are fighting over a woman, Susanna Moore. Wild Bill Hickok and Dave Tutt face each other at 6 pm on Market Square. Tutt fires first and misses but Hickok's shot takes deadly effect. [Wild Bill will later be cleared of manslaughter.]

September 23, 1865

In Helena, Montana, thief Tommy Cook is lynched by vigilantes [five more suspected Bad Men are rounded up and hanged within a week].

October 31, 1865

Bandits rob the stage at Geiger Grade, near Virginia City, Nevada.

November 10, 1865

Mark Twain and his manager are robbed on their way back to Virginia City, Nevada, from a lecture. Masked men get $225, two jack knives, three lead pencils and Twain's watch. [It turned out to be a sham robbery by six of Twain's friends who later gave back the loot.]

1866

The first cattle drives begin. Alfred Noble invents dynamite. Jack Daniels Whiskey is introduced.

February 13, 1866

"Missouri Bushwhackers" rob the Clay County Savings & Loan Association in Liberty, Missouri. As the gang escapes, an innocent bystander, George Wyore, is killed by gunfire from the fleeing outlaws. Although disputed by some, the gang is believed to have been led by Frank and Jesse James.

April 13, 1866

Robert LeRoy Parker [Butch Cassidy] is born at Beaver, Utah.

James Hickok: Infamous scout, gambler and sometime officer of the law.

Description: 6' 1", sandy brown hair, wears it long, scout style. Long flowing mustaches, favors Navy Colts worn butt forward. Known to have killed several men. Dangerous when drinking.

Alias: "Wild Bill"

(BBB)

JAMES BUTLER "WILD BILL" HICKOK

Arguably the most famous gunfighter the West ever produced, Wild Bill was the prototype for the standup shootist.
(BOB McCUBBIN COLLECTION)

HANK MONK, LEGENDARY STAGER
In addition to highwaymen, stage drivers had to fight the elements. Here we see Hank Monk dressed for the Sierra Nevada winter. In 20 years of service Monk never had an injured passenger. (AC)

April 14, 1866
Vigilantes in Sirup Creek, Idaho, hang their sheriff and a companion. The lawman, David Updyke, had been arrested and charged with "defrauding the revenue." He was out on bond when he tried to skip, but he didn't quite make it.

October 6, 1866
The Reno Brothers rob a passenger train near Seymour, Indiana.

1867

*Emperor Maximillian of Mexico is executed by firing squad.
Karl Marx publishes "Das Kapital."*

January 8, 1867
Congress approves legislation that allows blacks to vote in the District of Columbia.

January 25, 1867
The February issue of *Harpers Weekly* publishes the first article about Wild Bill Hickok. His fame as a frontiersman begins to spread.

February, 1867
After arguing over cards, famed bandido Narciso Bojorques, and One-eyed Jack Williams commit to a duel in Copperopolis, California. Each agree to exit the cantina; one by the front door and the other by the back, and when they meet outside they will open fire. Following the agreement to the letter, the combatants meet near the back door and fire: Narciso's pistol ball creases his opponent's head, but One-eyed Jack's first shot slams into Narciso's right arm, ricocheting into his heart and killing him instantly.

(BBB)

March 2, 1867

A Missouri outlaw gang is foiled in their attempt to rob a bank in Savannah, Missouri. The owner of the bank, Judge McLain, is shot [but recovers].

March 30, 1867

Secretary of State William Seward cuts a deal with Russia on the purchase of Alaska by the United States for $7.2 million in gold. Seward is roundly attacked for his "folly."

May 14, 1867

At Georgetown, Colorado, Ed Bainbridge is lynched for killing a "tinhorn gent."

May 23, 1867

An outlaw gang strikes at Richmond, Missouri, robbing the Hughes and Mason Bank. Six people are killed in the attack.

July 31, 1867

Despite his newfound fame (or maybe because of it), Wild Bill Hickok loses the election in Ellsworth, Kansas, for town constable to Chauncey B. Whitney.

August 2, 1867

Near Lake Tahoe at Echo Creek bridge, Deputy Sheriff James Hume shoots it out with members of the DeTell gang. Hume is shot in the arm, but kills one of the outlaws and captures another.

August 10, 1867

In a special election in Ellsworth County, Kansas, Ezra Kingsbury is elected sheriff. He will be affirmed as sheriff on Nov. 5th by defeating Wild Bill Hickok.

September 6, 1867

Three masked outlaws rob the Wells Fargo & Co. stage when it arrives at Desert Wells Station in Utah.

November 17, 1867

Wild Bill Metcalfe is lynched by a mob in Loma Parda, New Mexico.

ORIN PORTER ROCKWELL

In 1843, Mormon church founder, Joseph Smith, placed his hands upon Porter Rockwell's shoulders and prophesied, "so long as ye remain loyal and true to thy faith, need fear no enemy. Cut not thy hair and no bullet or blade can harm thee." The church had many enemies in those years and Rockwell became known as, "The Mormon Triggerman." His long hair, often worn in a braid, became his trademark for the next 35 years. Although active in his church he seemed to pick and choose the commandments he wanted to follow. He liked to drink and carouse in the local saloons and always ordered his drinks "squar" (without water), and when drinking would cry out "Wheat," which to him meant "good." Legend says he killed upwards of 200 men and managed to avoid a single physical injury at the hands of another man. Although the claims are obviously hyperbolic, his reputation was such, many of the men he went after believed it was true! An accurate tally will likely never be known because much of his activity was shrouded behind the protective shield of the church. While awaiting trial for murder in 1877, Rockwell went out on the town, came back to his room and died of a heart attack. Nearly 1,000 attended his funeral to hear Elder Joseph F. Smith deliver the eulogy, which said in part: "He had his little faults, but Porter's life on earth, taken altogether, was one worthy of example, and reflected honor upon the church." (LDS CHURCH ARCHIVES)

IDAHO STAGE STATION
Many stagecoach relay stations were quite isolated, like this one, and made easy targets for prowling gangs. (CHARLES SAVAGE PHOTO, AC)

TRES HOMBRES

Narato Ponce:
A noted ruffian and horse thief, the 35-year-old Chilean desperado came to California on a gold-seeker boat. Wanted for the callous killing of Bill Joy, an inoffensive old man who Ponce shot after a card game went sour at Hayward, California.

Aliases:
None known

Juan Soto:
Gang leader, robber and killer.

Description:
Over six feet high, well proportioned, and, according to the sheriff of Alameda County, "quick as a cat." Bear-headed, with long black hair, a beard, wears a soldier's coat and is known to be armed with two revolvers.

Aliases:
None known

Jesus Tejada:
Wanted for the robbery and murder of five people at the Medina Store in the Sierra foothills east of Stockton, California.

Description:
Over 6', devil-may-care look. Tall and erect, about 26-years-old, piercing black eyes, large hook nose. Considers himself a ladies' man. Carries one of Colt's largest six-shooters and a large, ivory handled knife which he tucks in his boot.

Aliases: None known

November 25, 1867
Alfred Nobel patents his invention, dynamite. [When he dies, in 1896, Alfred's will establishes the initial funds for what will become known as the Nobel Prize.]

December 15, 1867
In Pinole Valley, California, Chilean outlaw Narato Ponce is tracked down and killed in a running gunbattle with lawmen led by Sheriff Harry Morse.

1868

Congress enacts an 8-hour law for federal employees but most other workers continue to work 10 to 12 hours per day.

January 11, 1868
Three "gunmen" are hanged at Daly City, Wyoming (40 miles west of Cheyenne).

March 20, 1868
Vigilantes in Cheyenne, Wyoming lynch a horse thief and a killer.

March 25, 1868
A sheriff's posse out of Clinton, Texas, tracks two horse thieves to Bastrop, where one is killed and the other captured. The prisoner is then shot and killed on the return trip to Clinton for "attempting to escape."

March 28, 1868
Wild Bill Hickok breaks up a horse thief ring and delivers 11 prisoners to Topeka, Kansas.

March 30, 1868
The Senate impeachment trial of President Andrew Johnson begins at 1 pm. [The senators voted on May 16 and came up one ballot short, 35-19, of the two-thirds majority needed to oust Johnson from office.]

April 1, 1868

Arrested for a $20,000 robbery, Frank Reno and three others break jail in Glenwood, Iowa. Reno escapes into Canada.

April 24, 1868

In Viriginia City, Nevada, 5,000 spectators turn out for the hanging of John Milleian, who was convicted of strangling popular prostitute, Julia Bulette.

May, 1868

Near Salt Lake City, Utah, three bandits rob a stagecoach. [When they are caught several months later, they implicate a gaggle of well-known people in Idaho, Oregon and Washington State, including a former sheriff and two U.S. marshals. The sheriff swings.]

In Montana, vigilantes hang three outlaws and shoot another in the Lannon mining camp.

At Carson City, Nevada, a gunman named Jim Riley, kills Sheriff Tim Smith. A hard riding posse catches up to the killer on horseback, and in a running shootout, and with his ammunition running low, the outlaw commits suicide.

August 27, 1868

A mob in Laramie, Wyoming, hangs "a young ruffian."

October 19, 1868

The marshal's assistant, Steve Long, is strung up by a mob in Laramie, Wyoming, for attempting to rob and kill a prospector.

November 21, 1868

In Denver, Colorado, two members of the Musgrove gang arrive in town to rescue their leader, L.H. Musgrove. After several armed assaults and a killing, one of the raiders is killed and Musgrove is taken from jail and lynched. [The other "rescuer" is later caught in Wyoming, returned to Denver on the

BAD MEN HIDEOUTS

Every western local had a Bad Man sanctuary. Here are the most infamous locations. "There were numerous Robber's Roosts." Two are shown here. (AC)

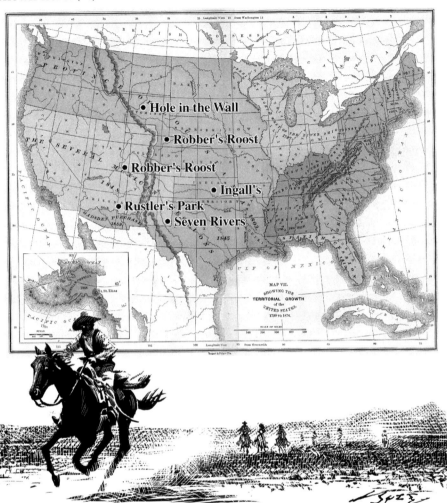

A RUNNING FIGHT

Stage, bank and train robbers rarely used their weapons except in a running fight, when a pursuing posse threatened their escape. If things looked bleak, some outlaws chose to turn their guns on themselves rather than be captured. (See May, 1868) (BBB)

THE HANGING OF "BIG STEVE" LONG AT LARAMIE, WYOMING

(BUFFALO BILL HISTORICAL SOCIETY)

NATIVE STAGE ROBBERS

Apaches rarely robbed stagecoaches, but when they did there were seldom any survivors. The great chief of the Chiricuahuas, Cochise, was the terror of the Butterfield line after the ill-fated Bascom affair (a blustering army officer, 2nd Lt. George Bascom, attempted to arrest Cochise for the kidnapping of Felix Ward—the future Mickey Free—see January 21, 1861) which set off a twenty year war. No stage was safe in the Arizona-New Mexico corridor for many years. To make matters worse, Anglo outlaws sometimes dressed as Indians and, or, left false clues at the scene of robberies to implicate Apaches and other tribes. Apache tribes often included half-breeds and blacks, as in the photo above, which were usually captured on raiding parties north and south of the border and assimilated into the band. (BOB McCUBBIN COLLECTION)

condition he won't be lynched, and when he is delivered, he is taken from jail and lynched.]

February 1, 1869
Outlaw Cullen Baker is hunted down and killed by a group of men who included his father-in-law. A Federal fugitive, Baker was leading a gang of men terrorizing the Dallas, Texas area.

February 8, 1869
Notorious horse thief "El Pollo" (The Chicken) is captured and shot at Socorro, New Mexico.

April 5, 1869
Ben Bickerstaff is shot to death by citizens of Alvarado, Texas, while hurrahing the town.

April 26, 1869
Vigilantes at Richmond, Texas, hang a suspected horse thief who had pushed his luck by stealing a good horse, selling it, then stealing it from the new owner and repeating the process. He is hung from a nearby bridge.

May 10, 1869
America's first transcontinental railroad is completed.

May 12, 1869
At Ellsworth, Kansas, an outlaw named Fitzpatrick is lynched for killing a man he found sleeping in a saloon after it was closed.

July 10-17, 1869
Marauding Apaches attack stagecoaches in New Mexico. Ten civilians are killed.

July 13, 1869
Anti-Chinese race riots turn bloody in San Francisco.

July 24, 1869
Rowdy Joe Lowe and Jim Bush of Ellsworth, Kansas, drug and rob a man in Joe's U.S. Saloon.

August 23, 1869

In DeWitt County, Texas, members of the Sutton faction ambush Hays and "Doboy" Taylor. Hays is killed and Doboy wounded.

August 24, 1869

Wild Bill Hickok is elected sheriff of Hays, Kansas. He shoots Bill Mulrey (Mulvey) who dies on August 25.

August 25, 1869

On his way to the gallows at Pond City, Kansas, outlaw John Langford confesses to killing six men. With that said, he puts the rope around his own neck and freely jumps to his death.

August 28, 1869

Three men leave the John Wesley Powell expedition down the Colorado River. They climb out the north rim of the Grand Canyon and are killed by Paiute Indians.

September 27, 1869

At Hays City, Kansas, Wild Bill Hickok kills Samuel Strawhim in a saloon brawl.

October 4, 1869

At Omaha, Nebraska, Wells Fargo officials agree to pay Lloyd Tevis $5 million for the exclusive rights to railroad express.

October 10, 1869

Wild Bill Hickok prevents a lynching at Hays City.

November 2, 1869

Wild Bill Hickok loses election for sheriff of Ellis County to Pete Lanihan by 89 to 114.

In Los Angeles, California, the northbound stage is robbed by three highwaymen.

November 17, 1869

The Suez Canal opens to traffic.

December 7, 1869

The James gang robs the Davies County Savings Bank in

BAD MEN OF THE FIRST WATER

Jesse James (above, left), at age 28, taken about a year after his marriage to his cousin Zerelda (Zee). Frank James (above, right), with hat in hand, about the time of his marriage. Notice the lack of similarity in their features, which leads some to speculate the boys may have had different fathers.
(BOTH PHOTOS, BOB McCUBBIN COLLECTION)

THE JAMES BOYS

Sons of a Baptist preacher who left, when the boys were mere tykes, to hunt gold in California, Jesse and his older brother Frank, were raised by their mother Zerelda. The James boys grew up in the middle of the Missouri-Kansas border guerrilla war amidst turbulence and lawlessness. Both saw action in the Civil War, fighting under legendary guerrilla leaders Quantrill and Bloody Bill Anderson. Jesse received a severe chest wound in 1865 but recovered. After the Civil War, both brothers evidently lived peaceably as farmers for a time, but they eventually turned their attention to outlaw pursuits and Jesse, at least, never looked back. Between 1866 and 1882, Jesse and Frank took part in at least 12 bank robberies, seven train robberies, four stagecoach holdups among numerous other highjinks (like the robbery of the Kansas City Fair receipts in 1872). They robbed and raided as far away as West Virginia and Alabama, Arkansas, Iowa and Kansas. But their bold string of successful raids would come to a crashing halt when the James gang picked the wrong bank, in the wrong town and in the wrong state.

JESSE'S ALIASES: Mr. Howard, Dingus (actually a nickname received during the war when a piece of equipment pinched him and Jesse cried, "Dingus!"—the non-word substitute for an expletive, stuck).

MOST PERSISTENT MYTH: The James gang robbed from the rich and gave to the poor.

ROBBER'S ROOST, 1870
Colorado stage station and former outlaw hangout near Virginia Dale, just south of the Wyoming border. The Roost could only be approached by a lone rocky trail and was an ideal hideout for Bad Men. (PHOTO BY WILLIAM HENRY JACKSON)

SUICIDE TRY FOR JESSE
Suffering from a chronic discharge in his right chest and depressed over the impending marriage of his sister to a man he didn't approve of (a Quantrill man), Jesse James attempted suicide by taking an overdose of morphine in early January, 1870. Thanks to the efforts of his brother, Frank, and his sister, Jesse survived the attempt.
(BOB McCUBBIN COLLECTION)

HELENA'S HANGMAN'S TREE, 1870
Proud vigilantes of Helena, Montana, turn to have their photo taken as their strangled victims, Joseph Wilson and J.L. Compton, twist slowly in the breeze. Evidently the two Bad Men were allowed a certain dignity, as they appear to have been hung with their hats on. (MONTANA HISTORICAL SOCIETY)

Gallatin, Missouri. Jesse kills cashier John Sheets and clerk William McDowell is wounded.

December 15, 1869
A posse of four men ride to the Samuel farm in Clay County, Missouri, to arrest Frank and Jesse James for the Gallatin bank robbery, but the brothers escape, killing one of the possemen's horses in the process.

December 25, 1869
At Towash, Texas, John Wesley Hardin shoots and kills a man who threatened him during a card game.

1870

France declares war on Prussia.
One in every four San Francisco families has a servant.
Texas is readmitted to the Union.

April 30, 1870
At Helena, Montana, a people's court overrules a district judge and hangs two men for the robbing and killing of an old man.

June 4, 1870
After being sworn in as city marshal of Abilene, Kansas, "Bear River" Tom Smith uses his fists to floor "Big Hank" and "Wyoming Frank." Within 24 hours, they and the town quiet down.

July 17-18, 1870
Wild Bill Hickok gets into a saloon brawl with members of the Seventh Cavalry. He kills one, wounds another in self defense. He is almost killed but can thank a Remington pistol which jammed for his extra time on earth.

August 26, 1870
In DeWitt County, Texas, Jack Helm, Bill Sutton, Doc White and John Meador arrest Henry and William Kelly in Sweet Home, Texas. Both brothers are shot dead. Helm claims they tried to escape but he is fired from the police.

September 12, 1870

The widow Catherine McCarty, arrives in the Wichita, Kansas area and takes a claim. She has two sons, Jose and Henry (Billy the Kid).

October 7, 1870

At Elizabethtown, New Mexico, rancher Clay Allison leads a mob into the local jail and helps lynch accused murderer Charles Kennedy. Allison then cuts off the man's head and places it on a pole in front of Henry Lambert's saloon in Cimarron, New Mexico.

November 2, 1870

Marshal "Bear River" Tom Smith is killed while trying to arrest a suspected murderer. Wild Bill Hickok replaces Smith as marshal of Abilene, Kansas.

November 5, 1870

Near Verdi, Nevada, the Central Pacific Railroad is robbed of over $41,000 in $20 gold coins. The outlaws, led by Gentleman Jack Davis, are arrested and $38,000 of the plunder is recovered.

November 9-10, 1870

Three suspected horse thieves are shot by vigilantes near Douglass, Kansas. Government scout Jack Corbin (who scouted for Custer) is hung, allegedly for being an accomplice, although no proof has ever been found to support the vigilante's claim. [Several weeks later, four more suspected thieves are hung for the same crime. The Douglass mob evidently was operating on the philosophy that given the law of averages, eventually they would punish the guilty parties.]

January 11, 1871

Near Waco, Texas, outlaw John Wesley Hardin kills four men (in a three day period) attempting to bring him in. Hardin heads for Mexico the next day.

SHERIFF HARRY MORSE

Unlike some legendary Wild West lawmen (see sidebar, opposite page), Sheriff Harry Morse of California was the real deal, compiling a stellar record that spanned five decades. Elected sheriff of Alameda County, California, in 1864, Morse, set out from Oakland, armed only with raw courage and a Colt revolver. He pursued a small army of Bad Men and beat most of them at their own game. He shot to death the notorious bandidos Narato Ponce and Juan Soto in two of the most classic gun battles of the entire Western experience. Morse also pursued Tiburcio Vasquez and his gang for two months and all but captured him (a local sheriff threw Morse off the trail to gain the reward for himself). His crowning achievement was the capture of Black Bart, the elusive scourge of law enforcement on the Western slope. An amazing record bar none. (BBB)

GOOD BAD MEN

"There is a thin line between catching an outlaw and becoming one."
—OLD VAQUERO SAYING

Frank Canton (COLLECTIONS, UNIVERSITY OF OKLAHOMA LIBRARY)

Texas John Slaughter (AC)

Pat Garrett (UNM)

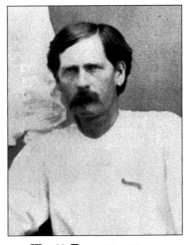

Wyatt Earp (JEFF MOREY)

For some lawmen, the line was too thin and the temptation too great. Tombstone Deputy Burt Alvord was one, evidently feeling he could rob trains better than the suspects he was trailing. Others, like Frank Canton (real name, Joe Horner), saw the errors of their youthful crimes (he robbed banks, killed several men) and tried to make amends. Most were complicated men, whose ethics and morality hinged on the lay of the land (although not of their era, "situation ethics" is a term they would have agreed with). Wyatt Earp was accused of horse stealing, embezzling school funds and murder, and yet, he was also a brave, efficient officer. Likewise, Texas John Slaughter was the first name on the list of outlaws the governor of New Mexico wanted locked up. Slaughter fled to Arizona, became respectable, got elected sheriff and is generally credited with helping to clean out the Bad Men from Cochise County. Pat Garrett was a bartender and gambling crony of Billy the Kid before changing sides and hunting down his former friend.

March 24, 1871
At Virginia City, Nevada, local vigilantes, calling themselves the "601," lynch Arthur Heffernan for murder.

April 1, 1871
Wyatt Earp and two others are arrested for stealing a horse in the Indian Nations.

April 30, 1871
In Arizona Territory, a mob of 140 Anglos, Mexicans and Papagos from Tucson, attacks a sleeping camp of Apache prisoners at Camp Grant, shooting and clubbing to death 83 women and children. The attackers carry off 30 of the children to be sold into Mexican slavery. The news of this slaughter shocks the nation and becomes known as the Camp Grant Massacre.

May 1, 1871
The first U.S. post cards are issued. They cost a penny each.

May 10, 1871
Sheriff Harry Morse corners infamous bandido Juan Soto in an adobe ranch house in the Saucelito Valley and, after a desperate gunfight, kills the outlaw.

June 3, 1871
The James-Younger gang robs a Corydon, Iowa bank.

July 7, 1871
John Wesley Hardin gets into a quarrel with Charles Couger in Abilene, Kansas and kills him.

July 18, 1871
In Hays City, Kansas, Sheriff Peter "Rattlesnake Pete" Lanihan is killed while trying to break up a saloon brawl.

August-September, 1871
At Hollister, California, Tiburcio Vasques and two others go on a crime spree, robbing several men and a stagecoach. All three are overtaken by a posse and in a shooting fray, one outlaw is killed. Vasquez is wounded, but escapes.

August 11, 1871
At Newton, Kansas, Mike McCluskie, alias Arthur Delaney, shoots and kills Billy Wilson, alias Bill Bailey. A fist fight gone sour started the fight.

August 20, 1871
Hugh Anderson shoots Mike McCluskie for killing Billy Wilson at Newton, Kansas, nine days earlier. Several others join in the shooting and as a result, Texas Jim Martin is shot in the neck and killed, Jim Wilkerson is shot in the nose. Two others are shot in the legs. This becomes known as the "Newton Massacre."

September 17, 1871
At Carson City Nevada, 29 desperate criminals escape the state prison, killing two in the process. Citizens form a posse and track the renegades to a lake in California where a desperate gun battle takes place. Three of the escapees are captured and two are promptly hung. Within two months 18 of the 29 are either captured or killed. Convict Lake received its name from this battle.

September 23, 1871
After an argument in a dance hall, Thomas Edwards walks up to the Newton, Kansas constable, C.B. King and places a derringer against the lawman's chest and fires. King dies almost instantly and Edwards escapes.

October 5, 1871
Wild Bill Hickok shoots Texan Phil Coe in Abilene, Kansas. Tragically, Hickok also kills his deputy, Mike Williams, as he runs to the scene. [Hickok mistook Williams in the dark, as a foe. Coe dies three days later.]

Geronimo: Bandit, raider and sometimes war chief, He-Who-Yawns (see below) is a ferocious fighter and gives no quarter in battle, or in Mexico.

Description: About 5' 11", muscular build, about 40 years of age, dark, piercing eyes, many scars (at least 8) from fights.

Aliases: None needed

GOYAHKLA (HE WHO YAWNS)
A Bedonkohe Apache who grew up in Western New Mexico and Eastern Arizona. He followed the great chief Mangas Coloradas (Red Sleeves) to Janos, Mexico, and it was there, in 1850, Mexicans killed his mother, his wife and three children. From that moment on, he hated Mexicans with a passion and killed scores to avenge the deaths of his family. A fierce fighter, he earned the Mexican-given name of Geronimo (after Saint Jerome) at a battle in Mexico. He didn't see a white person until 1851. Geronimo was never a chief, but a war leader. He escaped the reservation four different times, each time escaping to Mexico, until it became too hot down there and he would come back and surrender. After the fourth time, he and many others of his tribe were sent to Florida. On the day he left, the price of Arizona cattle ranches doubled in value. (PHOTO USED COURTESY OF GREGG ALBRECHT)

JOHN HENRY "DOC" HOLLIDAY
Photo taken in Philadelphia, when Holliday was about 20.
(BOB McCUBBIN COLLECTION)

November 5, 1871

Indians, believed to be Yavapai Apaches, attack a mail stage near Wickenburg, Arizona and kill six civilians [this becomes known as the Wickenburg Massacre].

In Ablilene, Kansas, the locals report that 700,000 cattle have been driven to town during the preceding season.

1872

John Henry "Doc" Holliday graduates from dental school in Baltimore, Maryland. Montgomery Ward opens for business in Chicago.

February 9, 1872

Notorious outlaw, Procopio Bustamente, is captured in a San Francisco brothel. [He is tried and convicted of stealing a cow and gets seven years in San Quentin. He gets out in five and resumes his bloody raiding until the 1890s when he is reportedly slain in Mexico.]

April 10, 1872

California bandido, Jesus Tejada, dies of syphilis in his Stockton jail cell.

Jesus Tejada (BBB)

April 29, 1872

Five armed men rob the Deposit Bank at Columbia, Kentucky. The cashier is killed and Frank and Jesse James along with Cole Younger, escape with $600.

May 23, 1872

The James gang robs the Savings Association at Genevieve, Missouri.

July 2, 1872

At Hartford, Connecticut, William Mason receives a patent on a new Colt revolver [which becomes the famous Peacemaker].

JAMES GANG DAYLIGHT ROBBERY
By the fall of 1872, The James gang was the terror of the Border States with their precision, lightning raids. (BBB)

August 28, 1872

In Niagra Falls, New York, Wild Bill Hickok appears in a stage show (and again on August 30).

In Kansas, Buffalo City is renamed Dodge City, honoring Colonel Richard Irving Dodge, the commander of nearby Fort Dodge.

Wes Hardin is again wounded by two state policemen but he drives them off with a shotgun.

September, 1872

On a hill overlooking Dodge City, the first body is buried in Boot Hill: a man known only as "Black Jack" who was shot by a gambler who went by "Denver."

November 15, 1872

The mayor of San Francisco exchanges telegraphic messages with the mayor of Adelaide, Australia, in ceremonies honoring the completion of the telegraph lines linking the U.S. and Australia via Europe.

1873

Silver is discovered in the Panamint Mountains of Nevada. Canada establishes the Northwest Mounted Police. Barbed wire is exhibited for the first time at the DeKalb, Illinois County Fair.

February 6, 1873

In Indian Territory (Oklahoma), two bands of Choctaw warriors capture 16 members of their own tribe, who they suspect of horse thievery. After obtaining confessions, they shoot and kill six of the outlaw leaders.

April, 1873

John Wesley Hardin gets into a quarrel with a Cuero, Texas deputy and kills him.

June 30, 1873

"Happy Jack" Marco of Ellsworth, Kansas, arrests Texan Billy Thompson for being drunk, disorderly and carrying a pistol.

MONTANA RANCH, 1872 (PHOTO BY WILLIAM HENRY JACKSON, NATIONAL ARCHIVES)

SPOTTING A BAD ONE

One of the conceits of nineteenth century society was that Bad Men could be recognized by certain facial features. On the day when career criminal Charles Mortimer (above) was to be hung—May 15, 1873—a doctor was dispatched to the prison to take his vital statistics prior to the execution. Dr. Brennan, a physiognomist, visited the jail and reported, "[Mortimer] is a man of small stature, but large and well built muscles; rather of a fine type of organization; gray-blue eyes, very close together; and the external orbicular ridge is contracted, so as to give him a sinister expression. The eyes are small and deeply set, as is generally found in most accomplished criminals." (AC)

Thompson, brother of Ben, is fined $25 court costs by Judge Osborne.

July 3, 1873
Citizens of the small town of Phoenix, Arizona, round up Mariano Tisnado, who allegedly stole a cow from a widow. He is lynched for the heinous offense of denying milk for a widow.

July 16, 1873
Stage driver Charley Phelps is shot and killed during a holdup near Malad, Idaho.

(BBB)

July 20, 1873
Near Adair, Iowa, the James gang robs the Chicago, Rock Island and Pacific Railroad, by derailing the train. The engineer is killed and the outlaws escape with about $1,700.

July 27, 1873
Four masked men hold up a Grass Valley, California, stagecoach and get away with $7,778 of Wells, Fargo money. [All four are arrested.]

July 24, 1873
Two bandits rob the Kelton stage in Rock Creek Canyon, Idaho and get away with $20,000 in gold coins and $1,200 in two gold bars.

August 8, 1873
Vigilantes in Tucson, Arizona, overpower U.S. Marshal Milton Duffield (famous locally for shooting Waco Bill) and lynch four men.

Robertson, CHEROKEE BILL MUSKOGEE, Ind. Ter

CHEROKEE BILL

Hailing from Fort Concho, Texas, young Crawford Goldsby (his real name) had a mixed lineage. His mother was half black, one-quarter Cherokee and one-quarter white; his father was part Anglo, Mexican and Sioux. He moved with his family to Oklahoma in the early eighties and he soon got in trouble, killing his brother-in-law at age 14. He was under suspicion for several other slayings when he joined the Bill Cook gang and assisted them in several store holdups and a train robbery. After his capture in February of 1895, he was sentenced to hang by Judge Issac Parker. After an aborted escape attempt, he was finally hung on March 17, 1896. (PHOTO COURTESY OF GLENN SHIRLEY)

(BBB)

MAKESHIFT JAILS

Frontier towns in the Wild West often grew faster than the municipal services could keep up. So, when it came to incarcerating Bad Men, sheriff's and lawmen often had to make do with what was handy.

THE FLOATING JAIL
With 5,000 gold seekers arriving every month, San Francisco authorities had to press into service a floating prison-brig, the Euphemia. (AC)

MEXICAN WOODEN JAILS
In the poorer parts of Mexico and the Southwest, where iron was expensive and hard to get, Mexicans built thick wooden jail doors. Of course, many prisoners set fire to them, prompting a neck ring to be added, which was attached to a wife or close relative. It didn't stop the burning, but it at least slowed them down. (BBB)

THE TELEGRAPH POLE JAIL
In Montana, one enterprising sheriff chained his prisoners to telegraph poles, which probably helped new arrivals: "How far is it to town?" "About three more prisoners." (BBB)

CAVE JAILS

Often, caves, mine shafts and cellars were pressed into service as makeshift jails. In Nogales, Sonora, a deep cavern saw duty as a municipal jail, and local tradition says Geronimo was once imprisoned there in the early 1880s. (BBB)

THE JAIL TREE

Before funds could be collected to build a jail, prisoners were often chained to a tree in the town square. Some of these trees became legendary, like the Wickenburg Jail Tree, in Arizona, which survives and is honored to this day. (BBB)

CLIFTON'S HARDROCK JAIL

Mining town Clifton, Arizona, took advantage of the local's mining expertise and blasted a jail out of hard rock. Ironically, the man who ramrodded the blasting was the first prisoner (he celebrated the completion of the job a tad too much). Unfortunately, the jail was right next to the San Francisco River, and when it flooded, prisoners were found treading water near the ceiling. (BBB)

TOMBSTONE'S WOOD SLAT JAIL

In the early days of the notorious camp, Tombstone had a small 10X12 foot wooden slat jail for prisoners. It was in this jail Wyatt Earp and others put Curly Bill after the shooting of Marshal White. Earp and others established a deadline around the jail and guarded the structure until daylight when the prisoner could be transported to Tucson, the closest secure jail. (BBB)

THE NAME GAME

Some historians claim the main reason we remember Billy the Kid, Jesse James and Wild Bill Hickok is because of their unique monikers. However, hundreds of Bad Men toiled outside the law during the golden era of the Western gunfighter and many went out of their way to make a name for themselves, but they are, for the most part, forgotten. Here's a partial list of the documented outlaws (they made the papers) who probably thought they had a handle for the ages. As you can see, it was not for lack of trying that some of these Bad Men aren't household names.

- "Snakehead" Thompson
- "202" (Will Christian's nickname, referring to his weight)
- "Club Foot" Lane
- "Rattlesnake Pete" Lanihan
- Charles "Rattlesnake Jake" Fallon
- "Little Reddy" Robert McKemie: also known as "Little Reddy from Texas"
- "Happy Bill" Chadwell
- "The Mormon Kid" (Harry Head)
- "Lame Johnny" Donahue
- "Coal Oil" Jimmy
- Adelbert "Bertie" Sly
- "Bean Belly" Smith
- Bob Bigtree
- "Blackie" Black
- John "Off Wheeler" Harlan
- Bladder Allen
- Blue Dick
- Jack Woman Killer
- "Mysterious Dave" Mather
- "Killin' Jim" Miller, also called Jim "Killer" Miller
- "Hairlip" Charlie Smith
- "The Catfish Kid"
- "Black Faced" Charlie Bryant (powder burns)
- Yankee Hank Fewclothes

- "Bloody Dick" Seymour
- The Pocked-Mark Kid
- Bull Shit Jack
- Slap Jack Bill— "The Pride of the Panhandle"
- Valentine Dell
- William Horseman
- Texas Jack Omohundro
- Dollay Graham
- Brigido Reyes
- "Cold Chuck Johnny"
- "Dynamite Sam"
- "Dirty Sock Jack"
- Johnny "Crooked Mouth" Green
- "Prairie Dog" Morrow
- "Acorn Head" Jones
- "Lengthy" Johnson (6' 4")
- Corn Hole Johnny
- "Beans" Davis
- "Alter Ego" Robert Strahorn (newspaperman turned Bad Man)
- "Red" McLaughlin
- Fly-Specked Billy
- Banjo Parker
- "Skunk" Curley

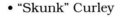

Ben Thompson: The English gunfighter.

Description: 5' 9", black hair and blue eyes. Quite a dandy dresser. Carries several weapons and isn't afraid to use them. No one questions his courage.

Aliases: None

BEN THOMPSON

No one questioned the courage of this English gunfighter. Born in Yorkshire and brought to the Austin, Texas, area at age 15, Thompson went to private school and studied to become a printer. But other pursuits interceded. He fought for the Confederacy and rode with the 2nd Texas Cavalry, fighting in several Civil War engagements, then transferred to Rip Ford's regiment patrolling the Rio Grande. In 1865 he was arrested for murder, escaped from jail to Mexico where he fought for Maxmillian and wound up a major. He returned to Texas and went into the saloon business with Phil Coe and Tom Bowles. He ran afoul of the law again and did two years in Huntsville, being released in 1870. After several more killings he was elected sheriff of Austin. He was extremely popular, except when drinking. (BOB McCUBBIN COLLECTION)

August 15, 1873
In Ellsworth, Kansas, Ben Thompson gets in a shooting scrape with two men, one a policeman. Ben's brother, Billy, who is drunk, accidentally kills Sheriff Whitney.

August 20, 1873
Ed Crawford kills Cad Pierce in Ellsworth, Kansas, in an argument over the killing of Sheriff Whitney by Billy Thompson.

August 26, 1873
At Tres Pinos, California, the Tiburcio Vasquez gang robs the Snyder Store. Three citizens are killed in the robbery.

September 15, 1873
South of Boise, Idaho, Harry McComas and J.B. Buckner rob a stagecoach [both are caught and sent to the Nevada Penitentiary].

September 18, 1873
A financial "panic" sweeps New York and 5,000 businesses fail [in a five year period].

October 17, 1873
Attorney Henry Ferris attempts to collect an overdue bill in the Slag Saloon at Akron, Colorado and is shot dead.

October 23, October 27 & November 1, 1873
Alleged highwayman, Shep Wixom, attempts to rob the Austin, Nevada stage three different times at the same spot. On the final attempt (Nov. 1) he is arrested and gets ten years.

November 10, 1873
The Tiburcio Vasquez gang robs the Jones Store two miles from Millerton, California.

(BBB)

December 1, 1873
Three Anglo men are drunk and shooting promiscuously at the locals in Lincoln, New Mexico.

Constable Juan Martinez, and others, attempt to arrest the men and a shootout ensues. All three Anglos are killed, as is Martinez. One of the dead men, Ben Horrell, is from Texas and has hotheaded relatives. This is the beginning of the so-called Horrell War.

December 18, 1873

"Instantaneous communication" between San Diego, California and Prescott, Arizona Territory, is inaugurated with the completion of the military telegraph line.

December 26, 1873

Riding 11 strong, Tiburcio Vasquez and his gang strike Kingston, California, plundering the town's two stores and hotel, tying up and robbing some 35 men. They escape in a hail of lead.

1874

*The Remington typewriter is introduced.
A group of French artists derisively dubbed "the Impressionists" have a show in Paris.*

January 2, 1874

The California legislature appropriates $500 for a posse to chase Tiburcio Vasquez and his gang. As an added incentive they offer a reward of $8,000 for Vasquez alive and $6,000 for him dead.

January 5, 1874

The first public school is held at Silver City, New Mexico. Among the 30 students is little Henry McCarty [the future Billy the Kid].

January 12, 1874

One mile west of the slaughter house at Denison, Texas, citizens hang a suspected horse thief.

January 15, 1874

The James gang holds up a stagecoach near Malvern, Arkansas.

JAMES GANG PRESS RELEASE

A note left at the scene of the Gads Hill robbery (Jan. 31, 1874) read: "The most daring on record—the southbound train on the Iron Mountain Railroad was robbed here this evening by seven heavily armed men, and robbed of _____dollars. The robbers arrived at the station some time before the arrival of the train, and arrested the station agent and put him under guard, then threw the train on the switch. The robbers were all large men, none of them under six feet tall. They were all masked and started in a southerly direction after they had robbed the train. They were all mounted on fine blooded horses. There is a hell of an excitement in this part of the country." On the outside of the note was written: "this contains an exact account of the robbery. We prefer this to be published in the newspapers rather than the grossly exaggerated accounts that usually appear after one of our jobs."

BILLY THE KID IS A KID

While the James gang is robbing banks and trains, little Henry McCarty is just starting school. He is seen here, in center, with two Silver City, N.M. pals. (BBB)

LOS ANGELES, 1871

It was in the hills outside this sleepy town that notorious Bad Man Tiburcio Vasquez hid out. Notice the fountain on the village square to the left of the Pico Hotel, with the fence around it. (WILLIAM GODFREY PHOTO, AC)

WILD BILL BAILS

Fed up with show biz, Wild Bill Hickok quits the Buffalo Bill troop at Rochester, New York. He was a poor actor, knew it and besides, he liked to fire blanks too close to the other actor's legs, sending them howling into the wings. Hickok is seen here in this publicity photo (second from left). *With him are Elisha Green* (far left), *Buffalo Bill Cody* (center), *Texas Jack Omohundro and Eugene Overton.* (BUFFALO BILL HISTORICAL CENTER)

EARLY HOLLYWOOD

This is a photo of the Jose Mascarel ranch, located where Hollywood stands today. This is the area Bad Man Tiburcio Vasquez was hiding out in when he was captured in May of 1874. (LA TITLE PHOTO)

January 31, 1874
The James gang strikes again at Gads hill, Missouri, this time robbing the Little Rock Express train.

February 26, 1874
Tiburcio Vasquez and Clodoveo Chavez rob a stagecoach and get $260 and a gold watch.

March 10, 1874
A Pinkerton operative, John Whicher (also Witcher) is killed when he attempts to penetrate the James gang stomping grounds around Kearney, Missouri.

March 13, 1874
Fed up with show biz, Wild Bill Hickok quits Buffalo Bill Cody's *Scouts of the Prairie* travelling show at Rochester, New York.

March 16, 1874
John and Jim Younger get into a gunfight with three Pinkerton detectives at Monegaw Springs, Missouri. John Younger dies as do two detectives.

April 24, 1874
Zerelda Mims marries her first cousin, Jesse James, in the parlor of her sister's home at Kearny, Missouri. Frank James elopes with Annie Ralston.

May 12, 1874
The James-Younger gang robs a stagecoach at San Antonio, Texas and get away with $3,000. [The James boys are married now and have to think seriously about their profession.]

May 15, 1874
Hiding at a ranch near Nichols Canyon [present day West Hollywood], Tiburcio Vasquez is surrounded by a local posse. Jumping out the back window of Greek George's adobe, Vasquez is brought down by a load of buckshot and captured. [The infamous prisoner is sent to San Francisco by steamer on May 23.]

May 26, 1874

Wes Hardin gets in a gunfight with the sheriff of Comanche County, Texas. Hardin and two friends, Jim Taylor and Bill Dixon, kill the sheriff and escape. [A citizen's posse later catches Hardin's brother, Joe, and two other Dixon boys and, even though they had nothing to do with the shooting, all three are lynched.]

June 2, 1874

The "301 Vigilante Movement" at Belmont, Nevada, hangs a pair of outlaws who had earlier escaped jail.

July 2, 1874

The Black Hills Expedition under direct command of Col. George Armstrong Custer leaves Fort Abraham Lincoln, [North] Dakota Territory.

July 22, 1874

Wild Bill Hickok arrives in Cheyenne, Wyoming.

July 27, 1874

"Acorn Head" Jones and two others are hanged in Kansas as suspected horse thieves.

July 30, 1874

Three suspected horse thieves are taken from jail in Wellington, Kansas and lynched.

July 31, 1874

Two suspected horse thieves are shot to death near San Saba, Texas.

August 6, 1874

Jim Reed, the so-called husband of Belle Starr, is shot and killed by Deputy Sheriff John Morris, near Paris, Texas.

August 8, 1874

One of Custer's scouts, "Lonesome Charley" Reynolds, arrives at Fort Laramie, delivering the news that gold has been discovered in the Black Hills. [Reynolds will die with Custer at the Little Big Horn.]

John Wesley Hardin:
A murderous, brawling, racist Texas cow-boy, schoolteacher, businessman (and eventually a lawyer). Legend says he once shot a man for snoring.

Description:
5' 9", weighs about 155 pounds, light brown hair, blue-gray eyes and broad, clean-shaven jaw.

Aliases:
"Young Seven-up," J.H. Swain, Jr.

JOHN WESLEY HARDIN
(BOB MCCUBBIN COLLECTION)

READY TO RIDE
A rare image of a Corrinne, Utah, posse getting ready to "git up and dust."
Photo is circa 1860s. (UTAH STATE UNIVERSITY LIBRARY, SPECIAL COLLECTIONS)

JOHN WESLEY HARDIN

Son of a frontier Methodist minister (he was named for the founder of Methodism), Hardin was arguably the most deadly gunfighter in the West. He killed his first man at age 15, several more by the time he was 16. In 1871, he went up the Chisholm Trail, killing five men enroute and three at the destination. He escaped custody numerous times, fought in several feuds, travelled widely and seemingly left bodies in his wake wherever he went. His grim tally was at 40 when he walked into the Acme Saloon in El Paso, Texas. He has been described as an intelligent man of violent prejudices. (BOB McCUBBIN COLLECTION)

August 11, 1874

Two outlaws rob the stagecoach at Mineral Hill, Nevada.

August 20, 1874

Vigilantes in Caldwell, Kansas, hang a man who had killed a cobbler in his shoeshop.

15 miles north of Denver, two men shoot U.S. Marshal Wilcox when he attempts to arrest them on mail fraud. After a long chase, Detective Dave Cook and Frank Smith arrest the outlaws at Pueblo, Colorado. Wilcox recovers.

September 21, 1874

A policeman, Flourney Yancey, who had been trailing the James gang, trades shots with two suspicious men near the Clay-Ray county line. The lawman believes the two were Jesse James and Jim Younger and that he wounded Jesse.

December 12, 1874

The James gang robs a train at Muncie, Kansas. [As an indicator of the gang's growing reputation, a bank is robbed in Corinth, Mississippi, on this same day and the James gang is blamed for both robberies.]

1875

The Kentucky Derby and American Christmas cards are introduced.

January 1, 1875

Doc Holliday exchanges shots with a saloon keeper in Dallas, Texas. Neither party is wounded.

January 5, 1875

Pinkerton operatives throw a flare into the Samuel farm home in an attempt to capture the James brothers. Dr. Samuel throws the flare into the fireplace where it explodes, killing Archie, Jesse's half-brother and blowing off the arm of Jesse's mother. Frank and Jesse escape.

January 23, 1875

At San Jose, California, Tiburcio Vasquez is sentenced to hang on March 19, 1875.

February 22, 1875

The San Diego stage is robbed. [This is the third California stage to be hit in the first two months of 1875.]

March 19, 1875

Before a large crowd of invited guests, Tiburcio Vasquez is hung at 1:30 pm. His last words are "Pronto! Pronto!" ("Quick! Quick!")

April 12, 1875

Suspecting a local farmer of housing a Pinkerton detective to spy on them, Frank and Jesse James, along with Clell Miller, ambush and kill Daniel Askew.

June 5, 1875

At Las Rucias, Texas, a squad of Texas Rangers, riding 18 strong, intercepts 14 Mexican rustlers and kill them all. One Ranger, L.S. Smith, is killed in the battle.

Late June, 1875

Wild Bill Hickok is charged with vagrancy in Cheyenne, Wyoming. He asks about the newest mining strike in the Black Hills and later travels to Kansas City to see about his failing eyesight.

July 5, 1875

The Fiddletown to Latrobe, California, stagecoach is robbed.

July 7, 1875

East of Otterville, Missouri, the James gang hits the Missouri Pacific Railroad.

July 26, 1875

Four miles from Copperopolis, California, Charles E. Boles robs the stagecoach enroute to Milton. [This is the first of 28 robberies committed by Black Bart.]

TEXAS RANGERS

The Texas legislature organized the Texas Rangers in 1874 to fight Bad Men of all stripes. This photo is of Ranger Company D taken in Realtos, Texas, in 1888. (LEE SILVA PHOTO)

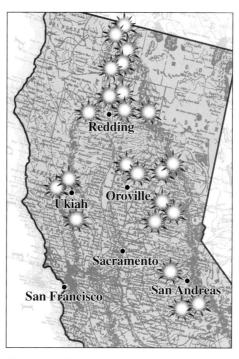

BLACK BART BEFUDDLES ALL

Nobody knows for sure how many stages Black Bart held up in his career. Wells Fargo believed he was responsible for 28 robbery attempts on their line alone. This doesn't count the many independent stage lines he may have hit! He seemed to have used four staging areas: Redding, in Shasta County; Ukiah, near the Shasta Ranges; San Andreas, in the surrounding mountains and Oroville in Butte County.
☀ *marks most of the known holdups by Black Bart.* (AC)

BOB YOUNGER, FARMER

The Youngers are prosperous farmers in Clay County, Missouri, although Bob and his brothers seem to be away from home quite often.
(BOB McCUBBIN COLLECTION)

Ned Christie:
Cherokee tribal councilman, blacksmith, whisky runner and horse thief.

Description:
Over 6', muscular build, long black hair, light facial hairs, broad cheekbones.

Aliases:
None

Ned Christie (COURTESY OF NATIONAL PARK SERVICE COLLECTION)

NED CHRISTIE

The notorious Indian Nations outlaw, Ned Christie defied posse after posse, until he was finally brought down by the posse members shown above. (BOB McCUBBIN COLLECTION)

August 11, 1875
The stagecoach from Soledad to Paso Robles, California, is robbed.

August 12, 1875
The stagecoach from Soledad to Paso Robles, California, is robbed again.

August 17, 1875
The stagecoach from Quincy to Oroville, California, is robbed.

September 1, 1875
The James gang robs a bank in Huntington, West Virginia and gets away with $2,000. [However, gang member Tom McDaniels is killed by a farmer posse and another suspect in the robbery is caught by Pinkertons and sentenced to 12 years in prison.]

September 3, 1875
Six men are hung at Fort Smith, Arkansas. All were murderers who committed their crimes in the Indian nations (Oklahoma).

October 2, 1875
Bandits in Arizona hold up the stage between Phoenix and Florence and get away with $1,400.

November 25, 1875
A former Tiburcio Vasquez lieutenant, Clodoveo Chavez, is shot dead near Yuma, Arizona, by Luis Raggio, who cuts off the dead outlaws head, ships it to California in an alcohol container for identification, and claims the $2,199.42 reward.  (BBB)

December, 1875
Wells Fargo Express officials report 31 robberies and attempted robberies in the state of California alone for 1875 with a resulting loss of $80,000.

1876

The telephone is patented.
One-piece-trapdoor underwear
(BVDs) are introduced in New York.
Heinz introduces tomato ketchup.

January 24, 1876

In a Mobeetie, Texas, saloon, Molly Brennan is killed by a stray bullet fired by one of the two men fighting over her. Cpl. Melvin A. King and Bat Masterson are the two desperate suitors. King is also slain. Masterson is seriously wounded, but survives [henceforth he walks with a cane].

March 5, 1876

Wild Bill Hickok marries circus owner, Agnes Lake Thatcher, at Cheyenne, Wyoming.

April 3, 1876

The California legislature passes a law stating that it will pay $300 for the arrest and conviction of each person found robbing a stagecoach or a train.

April 8, 1876

At Saw Log Creek, 15 miles from Dodge City, Kansas, two men are lynched on the suspicion of being horse thieves. [One of the men, John Callahan, was later proven to be innocent.]

April 9, 1876

Vigilantes out of Fort Griffin, Texas, catch a horse thief "in the act" and lynch him. Below the body they leave a pick and shovel for anyone who wishes to bury him.

April 14, 1876

Riding in Shackleford County, Texas, a posse including Sheriff Elect John Larn and John Selman, track down and kill four members of the Bill Henderson gang.

April 20, 1876

In Shackleford County, Texas, a horse thief is caught and lynched in a river bottom. On his shirt is pinned a note: "Horse Thief No. 5...He will have company soon."

BILL TILGHMAN

Born in Fort Dodge, Iowa, William Matthew Tilghman (above, left) was raised in Kansas and at age 17 commenced buffalo hide hunting. He was fearless and had numerous hair-raising escapes (he narrowly escaped lynching at Granada, Colorado, on a false-charge of murder). In 1876, Tilghman settled in Dodge City and operated a saloon although he was a non-drinker. He had numerous friends outside the law, including notorious horse rustler Dutch Henry Born. He married a local, Flora Kendall, who some claim was a soiled dove. (BOB McCUBBIN COLLECTION)

WILD BILL'S DEMISE

After Hickok's death, a miner's court acquitted his killer, Jack McCall. It was said the jury feared the local gambling fraternity of which Wild Bill was considered a member.
(BOB MCCUBBIN COLLECTION)

DEADWOOD, DAKOTA TERRITORY, 1876

Some say the killer of Wild Bill was captured at the Senate Saloon, which can be seen in this photo, half way up the street on the right side. (UNIVERSITY OF SOUTH DAKOTA MUSEUM)

April 21, 1876

At Fort Smith, Arkansas, five more men are hung for murder in the Indian Territories.

June 2, 1876

Vigilantes calling themselves the Tin-Hat-Brigade, hang outlaw gang leader Bill Henderson and Hank Floyd at Albany, Texas.

June 12, 1876

Outlaw Bill Longley escapes jail at Delta County, Texas and heads for the Indian Nations.

June 25, 1876

In Montana, Col. George Armstrong Custer and 188 men under his command are killed near the Little Big Horn River.

July 7, 1876

Riding at night, the James-Younger gang robs the Missouri Pacific Railroad at Rocky Cut, near Otterville, Missouri and gets off with over $15,000.

July 10, 1876

Wild Bill Hickok and party are on their way to the new boomtown of Deadwood, Dakota Territory. They will arrive tomorrow.

August 2, 1876

While playing cards at Saloon No. 10, Wild Bill Hickok is shot in the back of the head by Jack McCall.

August 3, 1876

A miner's court acquits Jack McCall for the murder of Wild Bill.

August 29(c), 1876

Bartender Sam Young kills Meyer Baum in a saloon on lower Main Street in Deadwood, Dakota Territory. Young claimed he was trying to kill Laughing Sam, an outlaw who the bartender feared was hunting him. A miner's jury finds Young "not guilty."

(BBB)

X Marks the Spot

The First National Bank of Northfield can be seen below the X in this 1876 photo. It was on this street the gang met a withering fire from the tenacious townspeople. Bob Younger tried to take refuge under the iron staircase (right, center), *but it didn't help: a bullet hit his elbow, breaking his arm.* (Northfield Historical Society)

First National Bank

A photograph of the robbery site taken in 1876. The timelock door, which unhinged the operation, can be clearly seen. (Northfield Historical Society)

We Are Rough Men Used to Rough Ways

Eight men rode into Northfield, disguised as cattle buyers. They were: (L to R), *Clell Miller, Bill Chadwell, Cole Younger, Bob Younger, Jesse James, Jim Younger, Frank James and Charlie Pitts.* (BBB)

Disaster at Northfield

After a long string of successful robberies, the James-Younger gang came into Minnesota ready to do a brisk business. Their guide, Bill Chadwell (real name William Stiles), was from the area and told them the pickings were easy. The banks were fat, he claimed, and the "Norskys" weren't expected to put up a fight.

As three of the gang entered the bank, everything that could go wrong did. The cashier would not cooperate and threw the gang off by claiming the safe was on a timer (it wasn't).

Outside, the townspeople had armed themselves and the ensuing fire was withering. Cole Younger was hit three times, his saddle horn and one of his reins was shot off, but he stayed in the saddle. While attempting to remount, Clell Miller was hit in the face and dropped dead in his tracks. Bill Chadwell took a bullet in the heart and died instantly as he tumbled from his horse.

The remaining six outlaws fled westward without their guide, or much to show for the carnage. Their withdrawal from the bank was a meager $26 and some change.

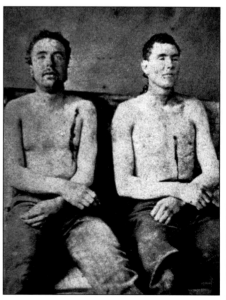

Clell Miller & Bill Chadwell
(Northfield Historical Society)

COLE YOUNGER

BOB YOUNGER

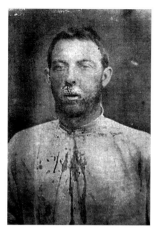

JIM YOUNGER

HANSKA SLOUGH SHOOTOUT

One of the largest manhunts in the history of the United States (over a thousand men were in the field to capture the robbers of the Northfield bank) came to an end at Hanska Slough (pronounced slew) west of Madelia, Minnesota.

As the posse closed in, the trapped outlaws were on foot, in a thicket. Charlie Pitts suggested they surrender, but Cole Younger boasted, "Charlie, this is where Cole Younger dies." To which, Pitts allegedly replied, "Captain, I can die as game as you can. Let's get it done." With that, Pitts stood and fired. A hailstorm of rifle balls was the reply, and Pitts fell back into the hollow, dead. The outlaws fired back, but the posse's firepower was too great. Jim Younger was hit in the jaw, the bullet taking out several teeth, while several bullets hit Cole, including one in the face, which lodged over his right eye. Bob Younger stood to surrender, saying, "They're all down but me." Another shot hit him in the chest and he went down. As the posse carefully moved in, Cole Younger tried to fight them with his fists but he was too weak. As a wagon hauled the outlaws into Madelia, the locals cheered their heroic posse. (FOUR PHOTOS ABOVE, BOB MCCUBBIN COLLECTION)

SHOT TO HELL
The aftermath of the Madelia shootout, left Charlie Pitts (below) dead and the remaining Youngers badly wounded. They are shown above, still bloody from their week long futile flight. Constant rain hampered their escape and kept them on the main roads.

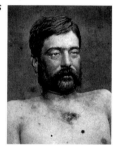

HOMETOWN HEROES
The Madelia posse who brought in the Youngers. (NORTHFIELD HISTORICAL SOCIETY)

JESSE & FRANK ESCAPE
Somewhere, near Madelia, the gang decided to split up. Jesse and Frank stole two horses and headed west, making it safely out of Minnesota and into the Dakotas, where some say they had relatives. From there they went by boat down the Missouri River to their homes. (BBB)

September 7, 1876
The James-Younger gang fails in their attempt to rob the First National Bank at Northfield, Minnesota (see sidebar).

September 8, 1876
At Fort Smith, Arkansas, four more men are hung for the crime of murder in the Indian Nations.

September 21, 1876
Bogged down in a driving rain, the fleeing James-Younger gang is pounced on by a posse west of Madelia, Minnesota. The posse kills Charlie Pitts and rounds up everyone except Frank and Jesse. Of the captured outlaws, James Younger has five wounds, Bob Younger has two, and Cole Younger has 11 wounds!

October 1, 1876
Texas Rangers attack the King Fisher outlaw gang at Espinoza Lake. Three outlaws are killed and another wounded. [Rangers kill two more outlaws in separate battles.]

October 20, 1876
Following California's lead, the Oregon legislature enacts a law that will pay $300 for the arrest and conviction of each person caught robbing a stagecoach or train.

November 7, 1876
Outlaws Johnny Ringo and Scott Cooley are broken out of jail by 40 men at Lampasas, Texas.

November 9, 1876
Pleading guilty at Faribualt, Minnesota, Cole Younger, and his brothers Bob and Jim are sentenced to life imprisonment at Stillwater for their part in the raid on Northfield.

November 24, 1876
Near Redding, California, in the third robbery of the month, the stage is held up.

December 4-6, 1876

At Yankton, Dakota, Jack McCall is retried for the murder of Wild Bill. This time he is convicted and sentenced to hang on March 1, 1877.

December 18, 1876

Eleven horse thieves are hung by vigilantes seven miles west of Fort Griffin, Texas.

December 25, 1876

Gunman Ben Thompson shoots and kills Mark Wilson at Austin, Texas.

1877

*Thomas Edison invents the phonograph.
Leo Tolstoy publishes "Anna Karenina."*

January 24, 1877

In the Dakota Territory, a posse of 20 men calling themselves the Black Hills Rangers overtake a gang of horse thieves and kill all nine. The Rangers are led by two men, one of them a 16-year-old boy named Fred Hans.

February 16, 1877

Following California and Oregon's lead, the Montana Territory legislature passes legislation that will reward $300 for the arrest and conviction of each person caught attempting to rob a stagecoach or train.

March 1, 1877

Wells Fargo & Co. announces that it will pay $300 for the arrest and conviction of each person engaged in robbing their express.

At Yankton, Dakota, Jack McCall is hanged for the murder of Wild Bill Hickok.

March 13, 1877

Chester Greenwood of Farmington, Maine, receives a patent for the first earmuffs.

THE ONLY KNOWN PHOTO OF SAM BASS, STANDING, AT LEFT (BOB MCCUBBIN COLLECTION)

SAM BASS

An orphan from Illinois, Sam Bass landed in Denton County, Texas, where he worked as a farmhand and teamster until he turned to horse stealing and robbing stagecoaches. In 1877 he and his gang held up a Union Pacific train at Big Springs, Nebraska, getting away with $60,000. A posse pursued the outlaws, killing three, but Bass escaped and made his way back to Texas, where he formed a new gang and began robbing trains around the Dallas area. After four holdups, Sam had little to show for his efforts, plus, lawmen had captured three of his gang and killed another. One of those captured, Jim Murphy, agreed to betray Bass in exchange for his freedom. He was released and rejoined Bass. The bank at Round Rock, Texas, was Sam's next target and the Texas Rangers were waiting for him. Ironically, local lawmen (unaware of the Ranger's presence) interceded and tried to arrest Bass and his party. In the ensuing gunfight, Sam Bass was mortally wounded, dying on his birthday, July 21, 1878. He was only 27.

AMAZING, BUT TRUE FACT: After his mortal wounding and capture, Sam told rangers: "If I killed Grimes [one of the lawmen he shot at during the Round Rock gunbattle], it was the first man I ever killed."

(PINKERTONS PHOTO)

Tom O'Day:
A Wyoming, Irish cow-boy and bank robber.

Description: Age 32, 5' 10" or 11", good build, 175 pounds, blue eyes, dark hair, rather bushy mustache, nose rather large.

Aliases: None

March 24, 1877
Sam Bass and four others attempt to rob the Deadwood stage. Driver Johnny Slaughter is killed.

April 8, 1877
Two men, one of them a "cardshark," are lynched by vigilantes at Rawlins, Wyoming.

April 12, 1877
Fred Hans, a 16-year-old, is attacked by five outlaws near Valentine, Nebraska. After they shoot his horse from under him, Hans jumps behind the dying animal, and sends a fuselage towards the mounted Bad Men, killing two outright and wounding a third. The other two surrender to the boy, who then delivers his captives 115 miles to Fort Sheridan. He doesn't sleep for 50 hours. The outlaws were part of the Bill Cole gang.

April 26, 1877
The Nevada State legislature passes a law that it will pay $250 for the arrest and conviction of each person robbing a stagecoach or train.

May 1, 1877
Three rustlers are hung by unknowns near Goose Pond, Texas. A placard on one of the bodies reads, "Cattle Thieves' Doom."

May 5, 1877
Sitting Bull leads his tribe into Canada, which he calls "Grandmother's Land," after Queen Victoria.

June 6, 1877
Bat Masterson is arrested at Dodge City, Kansas and fined $25 for hooliganism.

June 20, 1877
At Rapid City, Dakota Territory, three alleged horse thieves are captured. Two of them admit their guilt but claim their 17-year-old companion was not involved and had just joined them when they rode into town. All three are hanged.

June 25, 1877
The Deadwood to Cheyenne stage is robbed by five men who get away with $1,400.

June 27, 1877
Outlaws rob the Deadwood to Cheyenne stage line near the same spot for the third day in a row.
Near McDade, Texas, four men are taken from a dance and lynched.

June 30, 1877
The *Black Hills Daily News* reports more than a dozen stagecoach holdups for the month of June. There are also rumors of many robberies.

July 1, 1877
Wyatt Earp returns to Dodge City from Deadwood and stays about a week before leaving for Texas [where he will meet a certain dying dentist at Fort Griffin, named Doc Holliday].

(BBB)

DEAD STAGE ROBBER
Not all Bad Men were successful, as California Bad Man, John Keerer, found out the hard way. (WELLS FARGO)

BAD MEN ATTRACT GOOD WOMEN

The reckless ways of a renegade melted more than a few hearts on the frontier. Perhaps it was their untamable spirit, or maybe it was their freeflowing money (when they had it).

Many "proper woman" would never admit to a secret attraction to these outlaws, but the Wild Women on these pages not only admitted it, they often rode with "the Boys."

THE BEST IN THE HOUSE
When Kid Curry (above, right) showed up at Fanny Porter's bordello in San Antonio, Texas, he asked the notorious madame for the best girl in the house. Her name was Annie Rogers (above, left) and the two had a ball together.
(PINKERTONS PHOTO)

SUNDANCE AND ETTA
A handsome couple by any standard, these two rode the rails and the back trails together from the Wild West to New York and South America. What happened to the beautiful Etta Place has not been solved, yet. Some said she was a school teacher from Denver, others claim she taught a more physical therapy. Whatever her background she is a looker in any generation. (PINKERTONS PHOTO)

CALAMITY JANE
The notorious Western character, Calamity Jane, was a prostitute, scout and bar fly. She is seen here, with cow-boy Teddy Blue, sharing a beer outside a saloon in Montana.
(DENVER PUBLIC LIBRARY)

(DENVER PUBLIC LIBRARY)

WILD WOMEN OF THE WILD WEST

Rose of Cimarron (above), is a disputed character. Some claim she was a sweetheart of the Doolin gang at Ingalls. Pearl Hart (right) pulled off one of the last stagecoach robberies in Arizona with her boyfriend, Joe Boot. Della Rose (below, left) was a consort who ran with The Tall Texan of the Wild Bunch. Cattle Annie and Little Britches (below, center), ran with the Doolin gang and were captured and sent to reform school in Massachusetts. Belle Starr (below, far right), is probably the most famous female of the West, the most controversial and the least attractive.

(ARIZONA HISTORICAL SOCIETY)

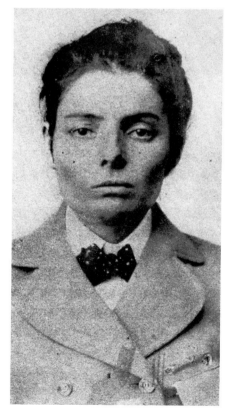

(PINKERTONS PHOTO)

(UNIVERSITY OF OKLAHOMA)

(UNIVERSITY OF OKLAHOMA)

CALIFORNIA CRIMINAL SLANG

*"Cross-man" Charles Mortimer wrote his autobiography
before he was hung in 1873 and it's full of colorful, criminal slang.
Surprisingly, much of it is still in use more than a century later.*

"screw and jimmy"—burglar tools.

"a trick"—a burglary job.

"to tumble"—suspicion, as in, "The cops had tumbled to us."

"good Indian"—an easy mark, or victim to rob, as in, "Pete spotted a good Indian for us."

"whacked up"—to divide loot, as in, "After the job Pete and I whacked up and separated."

"a narrow case"—a close call with the police.

"a frolic"—pulling jobs, as in, "I worked things lively and had many a frolic."

"pass in his checks"—to die, as in, "The shot did not bring him down, but if it had he would have passed in his checks."

"to outgeneral"—to outfox someone, as in, "They tried to put up jobs on me but I outgeneraled them."

"a cross-man"—a convict and criminal, as in, "A soiled dove asked me my calling and I admitted I was a cross-man."

"cases"—dollars, as in, "We need to beat this county out of a few cases tonight."

"fly"—inform on, as in, "He may put the cops fly and then we'd get collared."

"lamps"—eyes, as in, "You keep your lamps peeled on the place."

"hang"—to garrote, as in, "I think I'll hang that Injun up."

"gopher"—a safe.

"buck"—to tie up.

"swag"—a parcel of coin, or loot, as in, "This swag is heavy, take part of it and we'll whack it outside."

(AC)

"the cars"—the train, as in, "I intended to take the cars at Mountain View."

"the office"—a signal, or warning, as in, "She gave me the office—a cough—and went up Russian Hill to a dark, quiet spot."

"knuck"—a pickpocket, as in, "With her small experience in knucking, I told her I didn't think she could have got off scott clean."

"the dip"—to pickpocket.

"to stop"—stay with, as in, "I let Dick stop with me, even though I knew the detectives were looking for him."

"the ranch"—prison, as in, "The officers were all very interested in sending me over to the ranch."

"scruging"—dying, suffocating, as in, "If we put him in the gopher, aren't you afraid of him scruging?"

These terms were in use in the 1870s:

"detective"

"cops"

"stool pigeon"—one who betrays his kind.

"fence"—a person who will buy stolen property.

"frisk"—search.

"jail bird"—a convict.

"short timer"—a convict with a short prison sentence.

"shadow"—to follow someone.

"turning State's witness"—"I had oftimes of late been fearful that she might turn State's witness."

"slut"—"The slut will swear to it—I truly believe it."

Billy the Kid:
An unemployed bus boy who has been arrested several times for stealing saddles, tack and horses around Camp Grant, Arizona. Slippery when captured (he has escaped from the authorities numerous times). His real name is alleged to be Henry McCarty.

Description:
5' 7", 120 pounds, light brown hair, eyes have a roguish snap. Friends say he's so buck-toothed he could "eat pumpkins through a picket fence."

Aliases:
Kid Antrim, William H. Bonney, Billy Kid.

BILLY THE KID

Henry McCarty was his real name (How many movies about Henry the Kid would you go see?). He took the alias Billy the Kid sometime after he killed his first man (see August 18, 1877). Legend says he killed 21 men, one for every year of his life. How'd you like to be standing next to the Kid on New Year's Eve and he hadn't met his quota? Historians put his tally closer to five (in several of the gunbattles the Kid was involved in, numerous men were firing at the same person and we can't say for sure who killed whom). It has been claimed there are over 1,000 tomes to Billy, which, if true, would put him ahead of most U.S. presidents on the all-time best seller list. In spite of all the analysis, we're still not even sure where he was born, although legend says New York City. (BBB)

July 8, 1877
Jesse Evans and others are arrested in El Paso, Texas and jailed for, "filibustering" i.e. wholesale theft of cattle. [Around this time, Jesse forms a gang called "The Boys," which will include in its membership a young boy named Henry, riding under the alias, William H. Bonney.]

July 12, 1877
In California, Justin Arajo says, "I feel devilish and must kill somebody." He shoots the first man he sees and is lynched on the spot.

August 18, 1877
In Atkin's Saloon near Camp Grant, Arizona, Henry McCarty [the future Billy the Kid] kills Frank "Windy" Cahill. "I had called him a pimp," Cahill said in his dying statement, "and he called me a son of a bitch; we then took hold of each other; I did not hit him. I think I saw him go for his pistol and tried to get hold of it, but could not, and he shot me in the belly."

(BBB)

August 19, 1877
Stockmen from Arkansas pursue horse thieves into Texas, and when they overtake the outlaws in Red County, Texas, the outlaws, three in number, are hung from the same tree.

Mrs. Agnes Lake Hickok leaves Cheyenne for Deadwood to visit the grave of her husband, Wild Bill.

August 23, 1877
Killer and fugitive John Wesley Hardin is captured aboard a train in Florida by four lawmen.

August 25, 1877
In Arizona, Ed Schieffelin records his silver claim and names it "Tombstone."

August 26, 1877

Two citizens recognize members of the Shacknasty Jim gang as they ride into Deadwood. Sheriff Bullock and Boone May attempt to arrest the men as they leave the post office, but the outlaws break for freedom. Shots are exchanged as the bandits flee, but May wounds one before taking a shot in the arm. Three are captured and a lynching is barely avoided.

September 3, 1877

Outlaw Jack Davis is fatally wounded by Wells, Fargo guards when he and others attempt to rob the Eureka to Tybo, Nevada stage near Willow Springs.

September 18, 1877

Sam Bass and others rob a Union Pacific train at Big Springs, Nebraska and get away with $60,000.

October 5, 1877

Wes Hardin enters Texas State Penitentiary at Huntsville on a 25-year sentence.

(BBB)

November 16, 1877

Riding with six deputies, Deputy United States Marshal Seth Bullock raids a camp of "Road Agents" five miles west of Deadwood and arrests four outlaws.

December 24, 1877

On Christmas Eve, the Sam Bass gang robs a stagecoach at Allen Station, Texas.

Sam Bass (BBB)

Will Roberts:
A half-breed cow-boy (part Mexican) and train robber, age 36, height 5' 7 1/2", black hair and eyes, nose is good.

Aliases:
Dixon, Billy Roberts.

Other:
His mother is living at White Oaks, Lincoln County, New Mexico.

WILL ROBERTS (PINKERTONS)

JOHN WESLEY HARDIN
Texas' most feared gunman goes to jail. (BBB)

Frank Elliott:
A 21-year-old cow-boy turned robber. Height 5' 10", 160 pounds, brown eyes and hair.

Aliases:
"Peg Leg" Elliott, Bert Curtis, Robert Eldridge.

PEG LEG ELLIOTT (PINKERTONS)

THE OPENING SALVO IN THE LINCOLN COUNTY WAR

English rancher and merchant, John Henry Tunstall, was returning to Lincoln, N.M., when a rogue element of a Lincoln County posse attacked. As Tunstall's hired guns, which included Billy the Kid, fled towards a defensive position, Tunstall himself rode forward to talk it over. It was a fatal mistake. He was shot out of the saddle. (BBB)

BAT & WYATT

Two cool Dodge City policemen pose with their distinctive scroll badges. Bat Masterson and Wyatt Earp became lifelong friends during this period and it will be Bat who indirectly makes Wyatt a household name. (JEFF MOREY)

1878

The Edison Electric Light Co. is born.

January 26, 1878

Sam Bass and Frank Jackson rob a stagecoach between Fort Worth and Weatherford, Texas. They get away with $400 and four watches.

January 30, 1878

Near Kinsley, Kansas, train robbers "Dirty Dave" Rudabaugh and Edgar West are arrested by a posse led by Bat Masterson.

February 18, 1878

Rogue elements of a Lincoln County, New Mexico, posse overtake and kill English rancher-merchant John Tunstall. [This begins the Lincoln County War.]

February 22, 1878

Sam Bass and four others rob the Houtston & Texas Central express of $1,280 at Allen, Texas. [During the holdup, the gang used a Jesse James tactic: one of the outlaws raced through the coaches shouting that a robbery was in progress and that the robbers numbered "between 50 and 60!" Witnesses testified nobody on the train was overly anxious to test the accuracy of the statement.]

February 28, 1878

After a five-year lapse, the silver dollar becomes legal tender, again.

March 9, 1878

In a running gunbattle, a posse riding under the banner of *The Regulators,* captures Frank Baker and Billy Morton near Seven Rivers, New Mexico. The two captured men were believed to have been involved in the killing of John Tunstall. One of the Regulators is Henry McCarty, now riding under the alias of William Bonney, aka The Kid and Billy Kid. Both captives are killed on the return ride to Lincoln.

March 16, 1878

At Dodge City, Kansas, Dave Rudabaugh turns state's evidence on his fellow Kinsley train robbers and is released.

March 18, 1878

The Sam Bass gang holds up the Houston and Central Texas Railroad at Hutchins, Texas. Express car guard, Heck Thomas, hides $22,000 in a stove and Bass gets away with only $497.

April 1, 1878

Lincoln County Sheriff William Brady is shot and killed from ambush by members of The Regulators at Lincoln, New Mexico. A deputy also dies in the fuselage.

April 2, 1878

The Sam Bass gang robs the Texas and Pacific Railroad at Eagle Ford, Texas.

April 4, 1878

Led by farmer Dick Brewer, The Regulators try to arrest Andrew "Buckshot" Roberts at Blazer's Mill, New Mexico. Outnumbered 11 to 1, Roberts wounds Charlie Bowdre, George Coe and John Middleton, before killing Dick Brewer. [Buckshot Roberts, shot in the bowels on the first exchange of shots, dies the next morning.]

April 9, 1878

Lawman Ed Masterson is shot and killed in the line of duty at Dodge City, Kansas.

April 10, 1878

The Sam Bass gang robs the Texas and Pacific Railroad at Mesquite, Texas, getting away with $150, but not before outlaw Seaborn Barnes is shot in both legs.

(BBB)

DIME NOVELS GALORE

The Wild West Bad Man had his share of fans.

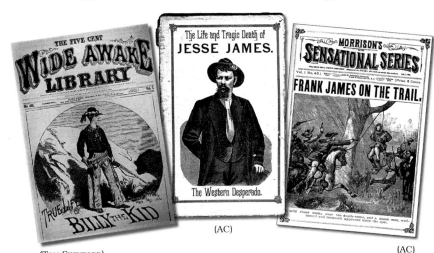

(TOM SWINFORD)   (AC)   (AC)

A traveller going by rail through Arizona in 1882 reported buying "a pamphlet purportedly to be an account of the exploits of Billy the Kid." Billy himself probably got a laugh out of reading the grandiose exploits of "Billy the Kid" in a serial running in the Las Vegas, N.M. *Optic*, in 1880. In fact many Bad Men read about their exploits in the *Police Gazette* and many other publications.

ELZA LAY
Colorado cow-boy, rustler and train robber. Butch Cassidy's chief lieutenant. Brainy and gentlemanly. Alias: William H. McGinnis. (PINKERTON PHOTO)

JOHN SELMAN
Texas gunman believed to have killed dozens, although hard to confirm. 5' 10", with dark hair, pale blue eyes, very cunning and persuasive. (BOB MCCUBBIN COLLECTION)

Jack Swilling: Known as, "The Father of Phoenix" for spearheading the rebuilding of the irrigation system originally built by the Hohokam Indians, this former scout and Indian fighter is a stellar member of the community when he is sober (which is increasingly infrequent). Recently acquitted of killing a man for voting the "wrong way." Rampant rumors claim Swilling "cowhided" a man for slandering a woman and "scalped" another man for unknown reasons. Currently under suspicion for robbing the Black Canyon Stage.

Description: Long, brownish hair worn scout style, between 5' 6" and 5' 8", many battle scars, needle marks on both arms from morphine addiction.

Aliases: The Father of Phoenix, Ol' Son of a Ditch.

Jack Swilling (BBB)

ELFEGO BACA

(MUSEUM OF NEW MEXICO)

He attended school in Topeka, Kansas, but at 15, was brought back to New Mexico, where his father was a sheriff at Belen. In 1884, the elder Baca was put in jail for killing two Anglo cow-boys and young Elfego broke him out. At age 19, Baca appointed himself a lawman at Frisco (Reserve), New Mexico and arrested a Slaughter ranch hand for hurrahing the town. In a standoff with the ranch foreman and his men, who had come in to free their comrade, Baca refused to give him up. Baca then counted to three in Spanish and began firing. Although no one was hit, the foreman was killed by a falling horse. In the confusion that followed, the young lawman then took refuge in a nearby jacal (a loose, wooden slat hut, dabbed with adobe) and was besieged for 36 hours by a large group of neighboring cow-boys who answered the call. In one of the most persistent assaults in Wild West history, the cow-boys poured thousands of rounds into the porous dwelling (the door alone being struck 400 times). When that didn't dislodge the lawman, fire and dynamite were used, both failing to dislodge the stubborn defender. Local tradition has it, that the next morning smoke could be seen coming out the chimney: Baca was heating tortillas and making coffee! The young firebrand finally surrendered to a friend but kept his guns, and was escorted to Socorro where he stayed in jail for two months. Tried twice at Albuquerque on charges of murder, he was finally acquitted. Impressed by his trials and defenders, the irrepressible Baca decided to become a peace officer and lawyer. He succeeded at both. (BBB)

April 14, 1878

Sweeping out of Old Mexico, approximately 30 marauders led by a white man, split into three groups and methodically plunder everything in their path near Laredo, Texas. About 20 men, women and children lose their lives as the raiders sweep toward Fort Ewell, gathering horses and booty at every ranch they raid.

April 16, 1878

A posse formed by Frank Gravis, gives chase to the Mexican maraured and forces them to give up much of their loot as they retreat back into Mexico. Unfortunately, the outlaws still get away with 200 horses.

April 19, 1878

Jack Swilling, one of the founders of Phoenix, Arizona, is accused of mailcoach robbery at Wickenburg. [Swilling is arrested in May; sent to Yuma for trial.]

May, 1878

Back in business, Dirty Dave Rudabaugh and several others rob a Kansas Pacific train at Rock Spring, Kansas and get away with $10,000.

June 21, 1878

Two men attempt to rob a Rock Island train near Des Moines, Iowa, while passengers are asleep. They get very little. This is the second attempted train robbery in Iowa within the past 30 days.

June 30, 1878

At Deadwood, South Dakota, Johnny Rogers kills Mrs. Neville in a pistol duel. Rogers is shot three hours later.

July 2, 1878

Outlaws attempt to rob a stagecoach in Whoop Up Canyon, South Dakota. Two road agents line up the passengers and start to rob them when a passenger, Daniel Flynn, pulls a revolver and shoots one of the bandits, later identified as John H. Brown.

Brown's partner, Charley Ross, alias Jimmy Patrick, shoots Flynn in the nose. A shootout ensues as the robbers shoot and wound E. E. Smith and A. Liberman. Flynn's nose wound is not serious.

July 4, 1878

Anarchy rules as the Rustlers, a group of outlaw raiders from the El Paso area, rape, murder and plunder their way down the Rio Bonito Valley in Lincoln County, New Mexico.

July 15-19, 1878

During a siege of the McSween house in Lincoln, New Mexico, four men are killed, including McSween. "Billy Kid" and others shoot their way out of the burning house and escape.

July 19, 1878

The Sam Bass gang rides into an ambush at Round Rock, Texas. Sheriff A.W. Grimes is killed along with one of the outlaws, Seaborn Barnes. Bass, who is fatally wounded, escapes, [but dies two days later, on his 27th birthday].

July 23, 1878

At Lightning Creek, Wyoming, the stage from Deadwood to Cheyenne is robbed. The outlaws reverently refuse to rob the Reverend J.W. Picket, but everyone else has to pay up.

July 25, 1878

Black Bart robs the Quincy to Oroville, California stage.

On this same day, several cow-boys are leaving Dodge City, Kansas and after retrieving their weapons they ride by and shoot into the Comquie Dance Hall and Theatre. Two policemen on duty step into the street and fire at the cow-boys as they ride across the bridge. One of the cow-boys rides off into the dark before falling from his horse. His name is George Hoyt and he soon dies from an infection from a shoulder wound. The two lawmen are Ed Masterson and Wyatt Earp.

THE REGULATORS

Although Billy Kid (the "the" was added after the war) shined during the Lincoln County War, he was not really the leader of the Tunstall-McSween faction. He was, however, fearless and a soldier whom the others in the gang (below), counted on when things got rough.

BILLY KID
William H. Bonney comes into his own during the Lincoln County War. (BBB)

Tunstall-McSween hired guns: (left to right) *Frank Coe, John Middleton, Tom O'Folliard, Fred Waite, Jim French.* (BBB)

TUCSON STREET SCENE, 1870s (ARIZONA HISTORICAL SOCIETY)

BILL BRAZELTON

Little is known of Brazelton's early years. He told a friend in Tucson he had robbed two stagecoaches in northern Arizona, three near Silver City, N.M., and four near Tucson (see July, 1878). Brazelton was described as "a great, big, good natured fellow; and except when on business, as harmless as any man could be." Through a turncoat, Pima County Sheriff Charles Shibbel was able to set a trap for the outlaw and, in a river-bottom thicket, the posse ambushed and killed Brazelton in a hail of gunfire. An ambulance brought him in to Tucson and they laid him on a table in the courthouse. Hundreds flocked to see the notorious Bad Man propped up with his guns and accouterments on.

Robbery victims reported that Brazelton held a pistol against the barrel of his rifle (left).

(BBB)

BILL BRAZELTON
The photos (above), *taken while the body was on display: one with his mask on, and one with it off.* (AHS)

July 30, 1878
Black Bart robs the Laporte to Oroville, California stage.

July 31, 1878
A Tucson to Florence stagecoach carrying three passengers, including editor John Clum, is robbed at Point of Mountain. The lone highwayman wears a muslin mask and favors a peculiar stance with his weapons (see sidebar). He gets away with about $60.

August 8, 1878
As the Tucson to Florence stage is approaching the spot where last week's robbery took place a passenger asks the driver to point it out. As the driver gets ready to point, out comes a lone masked man who shouts out, "I am here again! Throw out the strong box and give up your money!"
This time he gets away with about $500.

August 12, 1878
Jack Swilling dies in jail at Yuma, Arizona. The heat and unsanitary conditions combined with his chronic ill health did him in.

August 19, 1878
Outlaw William Brazelton is shot and killed near his hideout south of Tucson, Arizona. The bandit's body is loaded on a wagon and hauled into town where it is put on public display and photographed (see photos this page).

September 2, 1878
Bandits believed to be from Mexico, steal 500 pounds of silver bullion south of Tucson and kill two deputy U.S. marshals before escaping.

September 9, 1878
The Deadwood to Cheyenne stage is robbed by three bandits, believed to be led by William "Lengthy" Johnson. While the robbery is taking place the

northbound stage lumbers into view and is also stopped and robbed.

September 13, 1878

The Charles Carey gang robs two stagecoaches on the Cheyenne to Deadwood line. On the first stage the robbers take $10 from a male passenger but then give it back. A woman is left alone. When the second stage comes, one of the messengers, riding behind the stage, D. Boone May, opens fire and kills one of the robbers, Frank Towle. [Later May came back and dug him up, cut off his head and took it in to collect the $200 reward—it was never paid.]

September 26, 1878

A specially built stagecoach dubbed the "Monitor" because of it's steel plated body, is attacked at Canyon Springs, 35 miles south of Deadwood. Hiding behind and around a barn, six outlaws engage the Treasure Coach guards in a bloody shootout, before getting away with about $27,000.

October 2, 1878

Black Bart robs the stage from Cahto to Ukiah, California.

October 3, 1878

Moving down the road, Black Bart robs the stage from Covelo to Ukiah, California.

October 11, 1878

"Wild Bill" Longley is hung at Giddings, Texas.

October 13, 1878

"Duck" Goodale is arrested in Iowa for the robbery of the Treasure Coach on Sept. 26. He is carrying gold bullion and several watches stolen in the robbery. [Shackled and placed aboard a train to be taken back to Cheyenne for trial, he escapes and is never recaptured.]

BILL LONGLEY

A Texas Bad Man, Longley teamed with bandit chieftain Cullen Baker, raiding eastern Texas and into Arkansas. Later he worked a trail herd to Abilene and killed the trail boss. By the mid-seventies he became Texas' most wanted desperado. In 12 years some claimed he had killed 32 men. He was finally hung on October 11, 1878. He was described as six feet tall, 150 pounds, black hair and eyes, and had a piercing stare.

(BOB McCUBBIN COLLECTION)

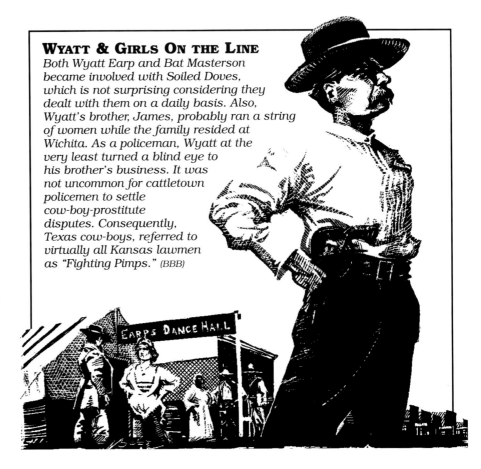

WYATT & GIRLS ON THE LINE

Both Wyatt Earp and Bat Masterson became involved with Soiled Doves, which is not surprising considering they dealt with them on a daily basis. Also, Wyatt's brother, James, probably ran a string of women while the family resided at Wichita. As a policeman, Wyatt at the very least turned a blind eye to his brother's business. It was not uncommon for cattletown policemen to settle cow-boy-prostitute disputes. Consequently, Texas cow-boys, referred to virtually all Kansas lawmen as "Fighting Pimps." (BBB)

TRAILING ON FOOT
The fiery son of legendary Sam Houston, Temple Houston (third from left), is pictured here leading a hunting party on foot. Many times in rough country, posses also trailed Bad Men with dogs. (OKLAHOMA HISTORICAL SOCIETY)

FRED WAITE AND HENRY BROWN
Co-horts of Billy the Kid, Fred (at left) and Henry, would survive the Lincoln Country War only to get into trouble elsewhere.
(BOB MCCUBBIN COLLECTION)

October 27, 1878
America's premier bank burglar, Jimmy Hope, with others, breaks into the Manhattan Savings Institution in New York and gets away with $2,747,700 in securities and cash.

November 1, 1878
Arrested at Grand Island, Nebraska, Albert Spears confesses to his part in the Treasure Coach robbery. Almost $4,000 worth of gold is found buried on a farm he worked on. [The outlaw is later sentenced to life in prison for his part in the robbery and is pardoned on Sept. 25, 1889.]

December 6, 1878
Four prisoners, mostly horse thieves, escape jail in Dodge City, Kansas.

December 15, 1878
A mob breaks into the jail at Meridian, Texas, and kills two men accused of murder.

1879

In Russia, Pavlov's dog is tested for conditioned reflexes. The first Woolworth store in Watertown, New York, opens for business.

February 10, 1879
The first electric arc lights are used in the California Theatre in San Francisco.

March 4, 1879
New Mexico Governor Lew Wallace makes out a list of 36 desperados he wants arrested in Lincoln County, New Mexico. Number one on the list is Texas John Slaughter. Billy the Kid (listed as "Kid Antrum") is fourteenth.

March 17, 1879
Governor Lew Wallace meets with Billy the Kid at Squire Wilson's jacal in Lincoln, New Mexico. The Kid is seeking a

pardon and agrees to submit to a fake arrest in order to testify against the killers of Huston Chapman.

April 5, 1879

At Dodge City, Kansas, "Cockeyed Frank" Loving shoots it out with Levi Richardson in the Long Branch Saloon. After a running gunbattle, Richardson slumps to the floor and dies. Loving is slightly wounded in the hand.

June 4, 1879

Murderer Manuel Barela and two others are lynched by a mob from the windmill on the plaza at Las Vegas, New Mexico.

June 7, 1879

Jim Murphy, betrayer of the Sam Bass gang, drinks atropine— some say for an eye ailment—and dies at Round Rock, Texas.

June 20-21, 1879

Two bandits attempt to rob the same stage twice, on consecutive days, near Marysville, California. The second time they are met by shotgun pellets fired by messenger George Hackett. One of the outlaws is wounded, both surrender.

July 9, 1879

Prisoner "Lame Johnny" Donahue, is being transported to Rapid City by coach, when vigilantes stop the stage and hang the stage robber near a creek that forever more bears his name: Lame Johnny Creek.

July 15, 1879

Near Folsom, New Mexico, outlaws rob the train and get away with $70,000.

July 19, 1879

In a quarrel over a saloon girl, Doc Holliday shoots Mike Gordon at Las Vegas, New Mexico.

(BBB)

MOONLIGHT MEETING

Governor Lew Wallace set up an appointment to meet one of Lincoln's most notorious outlaws. Wallace later related, "the door opened somewhat slowly and carefully, and there stood the young fellow generally known as the Kid, his Winchester in his right hand, his revolver in his left." (BBB)

LINCOLN COUNTY WARRIORS

These drinking hotheads are believed to be, (standing left to right) Jim Jones and Marion Turner (seated left to right) Bob Speakes and John Jones. The Jones boys were friendly with Billy the Kid, while the others were not. (MULLIN COLLECTION, HALEY HISTORY CENTER)

MYSTERIOUS DAVE MATHER

Born in Connecticut, Mather reached the Staked Plains in the early seventies, hunting buffalo before landing in Dodge City, Kansas. He was almost killed by a knife-wielding gambler, but was saved by the "first major surgery" in the young town's history. Like Wyatt Earp and Bat Masterson, Mather became a part-time gambler and part-time lawman, hopping the fence whenever he could. In 1879, he landed in Las Vegas, N.M., was acquitted of a train robbery charge, then became a constable. After several killings, he returned to Dodge and became an assistant marshal (when the above photo is believed to have been taken). After another killing and a gambling dispute, Mather left Dodge, becoming marshal of New Kiowa, Kansas, but he was soon off again and lost to history. His date of death is unknown. (KANSAS STATE HISTORICAL SOCIETY)

August 6, 1879

At Las Vegas, N.M., former Police Chief John McPherson shoots it out with Charles "Slick" Karl. Both are wounded. [McPherson dies on August 10th.]

August 16, 1879

Stages between Maricopa and Phoenix, Arizona, are being held up with such regularity that acting Governor John Gosper offers a bounty of $500 for every highwayman caught.

August 18, 1879

Dirty Dave Rudabaugh and Joe Carson are suspects in the robbing of the Santa Fe to Las Vegas stagecoach.

August 22, 1879

In Phoenix, Arizona, the Law & Order Committee takes two convicted murderers from the jail and hangs them on the town plaza.

August 29, 1879

Two outlaws, Colorado Bill Elliott and Dr. Henri Stewardt, are hung at Fort Smith, Arkansas.

September 1, 1879

Near Nevada City, California, the Eureka stage is robbed by two bandits, who kill a passenger and escape.

September 26, 1879

Fire destroys the entire business district of Deadwood, Dakota.

October 8, 1879

At Glendale, Missouri, an outlaw gang believed to be the James gang crew, takes hostages from a village store at dusk and commandeers the train depot. Forcing the agent to lower the green signal (which informs the train to stop) the raiders rob the Chicago and Alton railroad of some $6,000.

October 15, 1879

Masked men rob the Santa Fe railroad of $2,085.50 near Las Vegas, N.M.

October 25, 1879

The stage from Roseburg, Oregon to Redding, California, is robbed by Black Bart.

October 27, 1879

Black Bart strikes again, robbing the Alturas to Redding stage.

November 4, 1879

Two renowned gunfighters lose elections today: Bat Masterson is defeated for re-election as sheriff of Ford County, Kansas; Ben Thompson is defeated for city marshal of Austin, Texas.

November 14, 1879

Four masked men rob the Santa Fe railroad at Las Vegas, N.M. On this same day Dirty Dave Rudabaugh is named a policeman of New Town (East Las Vegas) by the notorious Hoodoo Brown.

November 19, 1879

A claim jumper and an outlaw are hung from the rafters of the jail kitchen by vigilantes in Leadville, Colorado. [It is gleefully reported about four hundred claim jumpers and other miscreants leave town the next day.]

1880

Lew Wallace publishes Ben Hur.
A vaccine is developed in Germany to combat yellow fever.

January 10, 1880

In Bob Hargrave's Saloon at Fort Sumner, New Mexico, Henry McCarty, now going by the moniker, Billy the Kid, shoots and kills Joe Grant.

PAT GARRETT DRESSED FOR A NEW MEXICO WINTER
A rare photograph of Lincoln County Sheriff Pat Garrett, taken in Roswell, N.M., in 1887. (UNIVERSITY OF NEW MEXICO)

A LIVELY AFFAIR
The first "legal hanging" in Leadville, Colorado, draws a crowd of 10,000 spectators in 1881. (DENVER PUBLIC LIBRARY, WESTERN HISTORY DEPARTMENT)

"Advise persons never to engage in killing."
—BILLY THE KID,
TO A REPORTER

BILLY BIDES HIS TIME

The Kid now gravitates between Fort Sumner and Las Vegas, N.M., gambling and rustling where he can. (BBB)

TYPICAL SALOON

Although this joint is at Fort Robinson, Nebraska, it could as easily be found at Anton Chico, or Puerto de Luna, where the Kid spent many a dollar and many a night. (NEBRASKA HISTORICAL SOCIETY)

THE INFAMOUS "HANGING WINDMILL" AT LAS VEGAS, N.M.
(MUSEUM OF NM, NEG. 14286.)

February 7, 1880
Three men accused of killing Las Vegas, N.M., City Marshal Joe Carson, are lynched from the local plaza "hanging windmill." In addition, the outlaws corpses are riddled with bullets (including several fired by Joe Carson's widow).

February 9, 1880
After a petition is circulated, the hanging windmill at Las Vegas is torn down as being a bad influence on kids.

April 30, 1880
Dirty Dave Rudabaugh attempts to break John Joshua Webb out of the Las Vegas jail, killing Sheriff Lino Valdez in the process.

May 15, 1880
Two men rob the Wells Fargo & Co. Express on the stage from Forest Hill to Auburn, California.

May 19, 1880
Jesse Evans and others rob the Sender and Siebenborn store at Fort Davis, Texas, of $900 cash and firearms and flee towards Old Mexico.

July 3, 1880
Jesse Evans and members of his gang are captured in a running gun battle with Texas Rangers near Presidio, Texas. One ranger and two of the outlaws are killed.

July 22, 1880
The stage from Point Arena to Duncan's Mills, California, is robbed by Black Bart.

August 6, 1880
May Killeen marries local celebrity Buckskin Frank Leslie in Tombstone. It has only been a few weeks since Leslie killed May's first husband, Mike.

October 11, 1880

Upset over being kicked out, Doc Holliday lunges back into the Oriental Saloon in Tombstone and begins firing. He hits owner Milt Joyce in the hand and an innocent bystander in the foot, before being disarmed.

October 28, 1880

Tombstone Marshal Fred White is shot in the left testicle while attempting to disarm cow-boy chieftain Curly Bill Brocius.

November 1, 1880

Virgil Earp is appointed assistant town marshal of Tombstone, after the death of Marshal Fred White.

November 2, 1880

In New Mexico, Pat Garrett is elected sheriff of Lincoln County.

November 10, 1880

Six prisoncrs, including J.J. Webb, escape from the jail in West Las Vegas, N.M., after apparently picking the lock to their cells. [A posse kills two, captures two, but Webb and another escape.]

November 20, 1880

One mile from the Oregon state line, Black Bart robs the Redding, California, to Roseburg, Oregon stage.

November 26, 1880

Sheriff-elect Pat Garrett and a posse are on the hunt for Billy the Kid when they capture escapees J.J. Webb and George Davis at a ranch on the Pecos River.

November, 27, 1880

One person is killed in a holdup of the stagecoach that runs on Black Canyon road into Yavapai County, Arizona.

December 1, 1880

Billy the Kid, Dirty Dave Rudabaugh and Billy Wilson are surrounded by a White Oaks, N.M. posse at the Greathouse

DOC HOLLIDAY SHOOTS MORE THAN HIS MOUTH OFF
Drunk and ornery, Holliday is getting into more and more trouble in Tombstone (see October 11, 1880). He will soon contaminate his closest friends to boot. (BBB)

THE WHITE SHOOTING
Marshal White (at left, above) attempts to grab Curly Bill's pistol as Wyatt Earp *takes hold of the cow-boy chieftain from the back. The gun discharges, sending a bullet crashing into White's groin.* (BBB)

Pat Garrett (above) *newly elected sheriff of Lincoln County.* (BBB)

J.J. Webb (at left) *in irons at the Las Vegas Jail.* (HIGHLANDS UNIVERSITY)

BILL MINER

Between 1866 and 1880, Miner was in and out of San Quentin three times, mostly for robbing stages. In 1880 he left the West, settled in Onondaga, Michigan and tried to live a respectable life under the name William Morgan. He lasted about a year. In March of 1881 he was arrested once again in Colorado for stage robbery. As he was being brought in he killed one of his captors and escaped. In the fall of 1881 Miner returned to California and took up his old habits. He was back in San Quentin by the end of the year on another stage robbery conviction, this time with a 25-year-sentence. On being released in 1901, Miner had a vow and a new nickname: "Old Bill" Miner swore he would never go back to prison. He was 54 years old and had spent nearly half his life behind bars. But old habits die hard, as we shall see...

(BOB McCUBBIN COLLECTION)

Ranch. In the ensuing standoff, Deputy Sheriff Jim Carlyle is killed but the outlaws escape.

December 19, 1880

Pat Garrett and his posse lay in ambush at snow-covered Fort Sumner, N.M., as they wait for Billy the Kid and his cohorts to come in. They do and in the ensuing fuselage, outlaw Tom O'Folliard is killed, but the others escape.

December 23, 1880

East of Fort Sumner, Garrett's posse surrounds the sleeping outlaws in a rock house at Stinking Springs. After killing Charlie Bowdre, the posse waits it out and captures Billy the Kid, Dave Rudabaugh, Billy Wilson and Tom Pickett.

CHARLIE AND MANUELA BOWDRE, 1880

(HAROLD B. LEE LIBRARY, BYU)

CLOTHES MAKE THE MAN

Bad Men, as a rule, didn't change clothing very often. When prisoner Charles Mortimer was brought into court at Santa Cruz, California, as a witness to the robbery of the County Treasury (almost a year to the day from the crime for which he was arrested) he testified: "I was dressed in the same coat and hat I now have on."

THE GRAY, THIN MAN
Given that most gamblers only carried "a suitcase and a trunk" is it much of a stretch to believe Doc Holliday (above), just might be wearing the same gray suit he is described as wearing by the myriad of witnesses to the so-called Gunfight at the O.K. Corral? This photo was taken in Prescott before he gravitated to Tombstone. (CRAIG FOUTS)

KID CURRY DRESSED AS A BUM
Harvey Logan, alias Kid Curry, as he appeared when he was arrested in Knoxville, Tennessee. Logan was a master of disguises. He wasn't alone. Jesse James allegedly carried a farmer's overalls with him on raids, as an effective disguise to thwart posses. Could he have been wearing such a disguise when he and his brother eluded dozens of posses in Minnesota?
(PINKERTONS PHOTO)

COMING AND GOING
Jesse James often went into town dressed as a prosperous cattle buyer or businessman and then fled as a poor farmer. An effective disguise to throw off most pursuers. (BBB)

Climax Jim:
Arizona cow-boy
and Bad Man,
wanted for
robbery and
forgery.

Description:
5' 9", long hair,
quite slippery
(escaped jail in
Solomonville,
A.T.)

Real Name:
Rufus Nephews

CLIMAX JIM

Fort Apache a.z.

CLIMAX JIM

Not much is known of this Arizona Bad Man. He is said to have showed up in Clifton area in the late eighties and did time in the famous Hardrock Jail (see page 31). Oldtimers say he was once a prisoner in the county jail at Solomonville, Arizona Territory and the jailers had the local blacksmith make a heavy pair of iron shackles and riveted them to his ankles. Confident of the results, the jailer remarked: "There, I guess these will stay on the son of a bitch." Climax Jim supposedly replied: "When you sons of bitches come back in the morning, I'll have these things off and a damn nice corkscrew made out them for you." In the morning, the jail was empty and the shackles were left behind in the shape of a corkscrew. (BOB McCUBBIN COLLECTION)

December 27, 1880

An angry mob confronts Pat Garrett and his prisoners at the train station in Las Vegas, New Mexico. The mob wants Dirty Dave because he killed a popular local, Lino Valdez. Billy the Kid offers to help Pat fight the whole crowd. After a half-hour standoff, a cohort of Garrett's gets in the engine cab and opens the throttle. After spinning in its tracks for several seconds the train rockets past the platform and leaves the mob behind.

By evening, Billy the Kid and the other prisoners are safely secured in the Santa Fe jail.

1881

*U.S. population reaches 53 million.
The American Red Cross
is founded.*

January 7, 1881

The Sedalia, Missouri *Daily Democrat* reports that Jesse James has been living in Denver and that he wants to come home and live unmolested. The, by now, legendary outlaw, also claims, to a reporter, that he attended the 1880 Republican national convention as a delegate from Mississippi and voted for Grant's nomination to a third term.

January 14, 1881

A young ner-do-well nicknamed Johnny-Behind-the Duece shoots and kills a popular mining engineer at Charleston, Arizona. A mob of mining men quickly forms. After removing the prisoner to nearby Tombstone to avoid a lynching, local authorities there are confronted by the Charleston mob before they can get him safely out of town. City Marshal Ben Sippy, John Behan, Virgil Earp and others hold off the mob with rifles and shotguns. After some tense moments, the lawmen finally get the prisoner safely on the road to Tucson. [Although none of the newspapers mention his name, Wyatt Earp is later given full credit for standing off this mob of 500 single-handedly.]

February 6, 1881

At Custer, (South) Dakota, "Fly Speck Billy" Fowler shoots Abe Barnes over a game of Spanish monte. A mob takes Fowler from jail and lynches him.

February 19, 1881

Luke Short kills Charlie Storms at Tombstone. They argued over a card game.

February 28, 1881

In Santa Fe, Sheriff Romulo Martinez discovers an escape tunnel and Billy the Kid is put in solitary confinement and shackled to the floor.

March 5, 1881

At Muscle Shoals, Alabama, the James gang robs a stagecoach and gets off with $5,000.

March 15, 1881

Outlaws attempt to rob the Tombstone to Benson stagecoach just beyond Drew's Station. The driver and a passenger are killed as the shotgun messenger, Bob Paul, returns fire. The stage bolts away in the dark.

March 22, 1881

Killer "Big Nose" George Parrott is lynched by a mob at Rawlins, Wyoming. [The outlaw's skin from his chest is made into a medicine bag and the skin from his thighs into a pair of shoes.]

March 28, 1881

Being transferred to Mesilla, N.M., for trial, Billy the Kid and his armed escorts are confronted by "six or seven roughs" at Rincon (end of track). The besieged group takes refuge in the back room of a saloon. Incredibly, some "disinterested men" succeed in dispersing the mob and the Kid party proceeds safely to Mesilla

LUKE SHORT

Born in Mississippi, Short came to Dodge City, Kansas, via Texas and, in 1870 took up the profession of gambler. He was quite the dandy and toured the Rockies with stops in Denver, Leadville, Cheyenne, Deadwood and Laramie before returning to Dodge. In 1880 he tried Tombstone and killed Charlie Storms in the Oriental Saloon. Acquitted, he returned to Dodge and more trouble (mostly political). Short finally sold out his interests in November of 1883 and went to Fort Worth. While there he shot and killed Bad Man Jim Courtright. Short returned to Kansas and died of dropsy at Geuda Springs on September 8, 1893. (KANSAS STATE HISTORICAL SOCIETY)

DALLAS STOUDENMIRE

A Confederate veteran from Alabama, Stoudenmire was named city marshal of El Paso, Texas. The April 14, 1881 gunbattle which Dallas took part in, brought him into a feuding relationship with the influential Manning brothers. Standing six feet, four inches, Stoudenmire was an imposing force. Unfortunately, when drinking he was ferocious and unpredictable. After another shooting, Stoudenmire and the Mannings signed a "peace treaty" but the bad blood continued. Stoudenmire resigned as marshal on May 29th, but on July 13th became a U.S. deputy marshal. On September 18, he was shot and killed by Jim Manning, who was acquitted. (UNIVERSITY OF OKLAHOMA)

THE TRIAL OF BILLY THE KID

The all Hispanic jury who convicted the Kid were given very narrow instructions by the judge: "If he was so present-encouraging-inciting-aiding-abetting-advising or commanding the killing of [Sheriff] Brady he is as much guilty as though he fired the fatal shot..." The Kid was then returned to Lincoln, and into the hands of his old friend, Pat Garrett (below).
(BOTH ILLUSTRATIONS, BBB)

via stagecoach. [It has never been determined whether this mob wanted to free the Kid or hang him.]

April 13, 1881

At Mesilla, N.M., at 5:15 p.m. Billy the Kid rises to face Judge Bristol. The judge directs that the prisoner be turned over to the sheriff of Lincoln County to be confined in jail until May 13 and on that day, between the hours of nine and three, "The said William Bonney, alias Kid, alias William Antrim be hanged by the neck until his body be dead."

April 14, 1881

In El Paso, Texas, a shootout between Constable Gus Krempkau and John Hale results in four fatalities. Dallas Stoudenmire runs to the scene and shoots a Mexican bystander [who dies the next day].

April 15, 1881

Doomed outlaw, Billy the Kid tells a reporter, "I expect to be lynched in going to Lincoln," adding, "Advise persons never to engage in killing."

Taking no chances, seven heavily armed lawmen accompany the Kid, who is handcuffed, shackled and chained to the back seat of an ambulance, for his final ride to Lincoln. They make the trip without incident and turn the prisoner over to Pat Garrett, who incarcerates the Kid in the Lincoln County jail (formerly the Dolan store).

April 16, 1881

Bat Masterson arrives back in Dodge City after receiving a telegram from brother Jim to come to his aid. As Bat steps from the train he sees his brother's enemies run for cover and he opens fire. Jim Masterson and Charlie Ronan join in and in the ensuing fuselage, Al Updegraff is killed. [Both Mastersons are run out of town.]

April 17, 1881

At El Paso, Marshal Dallas Stoudenmire and Doc Cummings shoot Bill Johnson after he attempts to bushwhack the marshal.

April (no date given), 1881

Club Foot Jack Lamberton is shot and killed by Tombstone lawman George McKelvey at Charleston, Arizona, while attempting to rob a stagecoach.

April 28, 1881

Billy the Kid kills two of his jailers and escapes hanging in Lincoln, New Mexico.

May 13, 1881

At Fronteras, Sonora, Mexico, four American cow-boys from Galeyville, Arizona, are shot down.

May, 1881

The Charlie Allison gang has robbed five stagecoaches around Alamosa, Colorado. Now they turn their attention to New Mexico and plunder the town of Chama.

May 25, 1881

Drunk and in a dangerous mood, Curly Bill Brocius is shot in the neck by one of his cow-boy cohorts at Galeyville, Arizona. The bullet exits out his right cheek and, incredibly, he survives.

June 6, 1881

Known stage robbers, Bill Leonard and Harry Head are killed while attempting to rob a store in the Bootheel of New Mexico. [Several days later, friends of Leonard and Head kill the store owners.]

June 18, 1881

The leader of the Charlie Allison gang and two others are arrested in Albuquerque, N.M., and extradited to Colorado for trial.

June 24, 1881

An Alamosa, Colorado, mob attempts to lynch Charlie Allison and his fellow gang members, but

Curly Bill Brocius: The so-called "Captain of the Cow-boys" is under suspicion for numerous forays into Old Mexico on stock stealing raids. Known to wear "two belts of cartridges, a revolver and carry a Henry rifle in his hand." According to Tombstone Deputy Billy Breakenridge, Curly Bill is "a remarkable shot with a pistol," and can "hit a rabbit every time when it is running thirty or forty yards away."

Description: A husky, six footer with black, curly hair, and a freckled face. Some who know him say he favors a "red tie."

Aliases: William Graham, William Rogers

CURLY BILL BROCIUS (ALSO SPELLED BROSCIOU)

Hailing from Texas (some say Missouri), Curly Bill came to Arizona in 1878 with a herd of cattle bound for the San Carlos Apache reservation. Afterwards, Bill drifted into southeastern Arizona and fell in with the numerous Texas cow-boys around Rustler's Park in the Chiricuahuas. Friends described him as "jolly." His favorite haunts were Galeyville and San Simon, Shakespeare, N.M., and he also enjoyed the faro tables in Tombstone and Charleston. Curly Bill and his gang were said to have waylaid numerous Mexican pack trains in Skeleton Canyon, but there are many who think these tales are highly overdrawn. Thanks to Wyatt Earp, who testified on Curly Bill's behalf, Brocius was cleared at Tucson for the shooting death of Marshal White (see October 28, 1880) and released after spending several months in jail. Bedridden for several months after being shot in the jaw (see May 25, 1881), Curly Bill received a poignant warning from one of his doomed outlaw comrades (see opposite page). By the summer of 1881 Brocius was said to have left Arizona, bound for Texas "to see my mother," and was reported not to have returned to Arizona. For years, there were reports from oldtimers who claimed to have seen the aging outlaw in Colorado, Wyoming, Montana, Texas and Old Mexico. One insisted he died of the German measles, another said he had a big family in Mexico, still another claimed Bill lived until World War II. (No known photo of Brocius has been found.) Of course, Wyatt Earp claimed he killed the outlaw at Mescal Springs. The Tombstone papers had a lively debate about Curly Bill's aliveness, each offering sizeable rewards for proof of his life or death. Neither side was ever satisfied. (BBB)

A WARNING FOR CURLY BILL

Arizona outlaw Tom Harper had been convicted of killing an unarmed, old man in a dispute over money. On July 8, 1881, just before he was hung, he gave a poignant warning to his friend, Curly Bill Brocius: "Curly, you are aware that I am not in the habit of lecturing any man, but in this case you may remember the words of a dying man (for I am all to intents and purposes such), and perhaps give heed to them...Curly, I want you to take warning by me. Do not be too handy with a pistol. Keep cool and never fire at a man unless in the actual defense of your life. You must stand a heap from a man before

THE HANGING OF FERAMINI
(ARIZONA HISTORICAL SOCIETY)

you kill him. Words do not hurt, so you must never mind what is said to aggravate you. As I said before, don't try and hunt a row. Give my kind regards to any of my old friends who you may chance to meet, and tell them to take a warning by me. I bear no ill will, and I think I am going to die in peace. Hoping you will take heed of what I write, I am, as ever, your unfortunate friend."
— Thomas Harper, *Arizona Mining Journal*, July 9, 1881

Frank McLaury
(BBB)

Old Man Clanton
(BOB MCCUBBIN COLLECTION)

lawmen remove the prisoners to Denver. [Allison and the others are eventually returned to Alamosa, tried, convicted and sentenced to 35 years in the pen.]

July 8, 1881
Outlaw Tom Harper is led to the gallows at Tucson, Arizona. As his last statement, he warns his friend and fellow Bad Man Curly Bill Brocius to quit the outlaw life before it's too late. (See statement at left).

July 11, 1881
Four men rob the Riverton, Iowa, Davis and Sexton Bank and get away with $4,000. [The James gang is immediately suspected of the job, but it is later determined the robbery was the work of an outlaw band led by Polk Wells.]

July 14, 1881
At Fort Sumner, New Mexico, Sheriff Pat Garrett ambushes Billy the Kid in a darkened bedroom and kills him.

July 15, 1881
The James gang holds up the Chicago, Rock Island Pacific Railroad at Winston, Missouri. The conductor and a civilian are murdered in the robbery. The outlaws loot the express car safe and escape.

July 28, 1881
Missouri Governor Thomas Crittendon offers a $5,000 reward each for Frank and Jesse James.

August 13, 1881
Within sight of the Mexican border, Old Man Clanton and four other cow-boys are ambushed and killed at Gudalupe Canyon, Arizona. It is believed the killing is in retaliation for previous rustler excursions into Mexico.

August 24, 1881
Outlaw Burt Wilkinson kills a Silverton, Colorado, lawman while resisting arrest. A large reward (some say $2,500) is offered and

Wilkinson is subsequently captured by his own gang members, Ike Stockton and Bud Galbreth, who collect!

August 31, 1881
Black Bart robs the Yreka, California stage, nine miles from town.

September 4, 1881
Burt Wilkinson is lynched at Silverton.

September 7, 1881
The James gang robs the Chicago and Alton Railroad at Blue Cut, Missouri. All the raiders are masked except one; a tall, black-bearded man, who boasts loudly he is Jesse James and that this attack is to avenge the railroad's participation in the reward for his capture. After plundering the express box, the outlaws systematically rob most of the 90 plus passengers and get away with some $12,000.

September 8, 1881
The Tombstone to Bisbee stage is held up near Hereford, Arizona, and outlaws get away with over $3,250 in cash and jewelry. [One of the suspects turns out to be Deputy Sheriff Frank Stillwell.]

September 9, 1881
Five outlaws are hung at Fort Smith, Arkansas, for crimes committed in the Indian Nations (Oklahoma).

September 26, 1881
Durango, Colorado lawmen arrest Ike Stockton and Bud Galbreth, but Stockton reaches for his gun and is shot in the upper thigh. [Stockton dies the next day after his leg is amputated.]

October 7, 1881
Two former members of the Ike Stockton gang are lynched at Socorro, New Mexico.

A MISDEMEANOR ARREST GONE AWRY

The events of October 26, 1881 basically boil down to this:

- At approximately 2:30 pm on a cold, blustery day, City Marhsal Virgil Earp, his brothers Wyatt and Morgan, along with Doc Holliday confronted a group of hostile cow-boys in a narrow, vacant lot on Fremont Street.

- Witnesses testified over 30 shots were fired in about 30 seconds.

- The cow-boys (and friendly witnesses) claimed the Earps fired five shots before the cow-boys returned fire.

- The Earps claimed Wyatt and Billy Clanton fired at the same time.

- When it was over, three of the cow-boys were dead and two of the Earps wounded.

- The Earps were acquitted at a subsequent hearing.

- The repercussions would last a little longer.

(ALL ILLUSTRATIONS, BBB)

Russian Bill: A wannabe Bad Man. Locals claim suspect "swaggers in tombstone," is "tolerated by Curly Bill and Johnny Ringo," and that he at one time worked for the McLaurys.

Description: A "gangling man of blonde complexion," standing over 6' 2" in height.

RUSSIAN BILL SWINGS

His real name was William Rogers Tettenborn and he hailed from a Baltic Sea port and claimed Russian nobility in his lineage. He landed at San Francisco sometime in the seventies, travelling inland from there, before landing at Fort Worth, Texas, where he was wounded in a gunfight. He allegedly was in Denver, Colorado, for a time before landing in the bootheel of New Mexico, where he fell in with "the cow-boy element." Bad Man Sandy King became Russian Bill's mentor and the two took part in numerous escapades and minor outlawry. In early November, 1881, King, also known as Red Curly, and Russian Bill were in a hard fought battle with Arizona ranchers who were tired of losing stock to outlaw predators. Deputy Sheriff Dan Tucker, operating out of Deming, New Mexico, captured Russian Bill on a stolen horse and returned him to the Shakespeare, N.M., jail. There he was joined by Sandy King who had shot the tip off a clerk's finger for fun. Locals were "damned tired" of the two and at 2 am on November 9th, in the small village of Shakespeare (south of present day Lordsburg) the two outlaws were strung up from the rafters in the barroom of the Shakespeare Hotel. Local lore claims King was hung for his many outlaw deeds and Bill was strung up with him "because he was a damned nuisance." (BBB)

October 8, 1881
Black Bart robs the Yreka to Redding, California, stage.

October 11, 1881
The stage from Lakeview to Redding, California, is robbed by Black Bart.

October 26, 1881
The Earp brothers with Doc Holliday shoot it out with the McLaurys and Clantons in a vacant lot on Fremont Street in Tombstone, Arizona. Three of the cow-boys are killed.

November 7, 1881
Bill Miner and his gang rob the stage near Sonora, California. [Miner and two gang members are captured and sent to San Quentin.]

November 8, 1881
Tom Howard (Jesse James) and family rent a house in Saint Joseph, Missouri, for $14 a month.

November 9, 1881
Sandy King and Russian Bill are taken from the Shakespeare, New Mexico, jail and lynched from the barroom rafters of the Shakespeare Hotel.

December 3, 1881
Dirty Dave Rudabaugh and six others successfully dig their way out of the Las Vegas, N.M., jail and escape.

December 4, 1881
James gang members, Dick Liddil and Wood Hite (Jesse James' cousin) have an argument over a woman (others say over the way the Blue Cut robbery money had been divided). Bob Ford intervenes and kills Hite. Ford and Liddil bury the body in a horse blanket and Liddil decides to turn himself in to the authorities, partly to avoid the wrath of Jesse. (BBB)

December 15, 1881

Four miles from Dobbin's Ranch, Black Bart robs the Downieville to Marysville, California, stage.

December 17, 1881

In a wild shootout at Caldwell, Kansas, the Jim Talbot gang shoots and kills Mike Meagher, while losing one of their own.

December 27, 1881

The stage from North San Juan to Smartsville, California is robbed by Black Bart.

December 28, 1881

A half-hour before midnight, City Marshal Virgil Earp is shot by concealed assassins as he crosses Fifth Street in Tombstone. Two doctors work into the night to save his life, finally, sawing off several inches of his left humerus (the bone between the shoulder and elbow).

1882

The Hatfield-McCoy feud breaks out in West Virginia.
British gunboats bombard Alexandria in the opening of the Anglo-Egyptian War.

January 5, 1882

Four miles west of Copperopolis, California, the stage is robbed. [The local sheriff arrests a 22-year-old from New York who is carrying a black mask, two pistols, a bowie knife and a book entitled "Lives of Vasques, Murrieta and Billy the Kid."

January 7, 1882

The Benson to Tombstone stage is robbed.

January 24, 1882

Dick Liddil surrenders to Clay County, Missouri, Sheriff James Timberlake and with the outlaw's inside information (in addition to Clarence Hite's confession), law

Doc Holliday:
Troublesome, ornery, he is allegedly dying of consumption and is wont to seek a violent end to his life. He has been going out of his way to die with his boots on in Prescott, Gillette, Tucson, Contention, Charleston and Tombstone. Has certain friends in law enforcement.

Description:
6' 0", 135 pounds, tall and gaunt, sandy blond hair, speaks with a Southern twang, intelligent, belligerent when drinking (seldom sober).

Aliases:
Too drunk to bother.

DOC HOLLIDAY: DRUNK AS A SKUNK!

The good doctor was known to drink quite heavily and most, if not all, the trouble he got into could be directly traceable to being soused. (BBB)

DRUNK & DISORDERLY

Most Bad Men drank to excess and in many cases it was their undoing. California career criminal, Charles Mortimer, admitted, "I had become habituated to the use of liquor, and it often threw me out of work. I tried hard to stop drinking, but never fully succeeded, nor from keeping away from old associates."

There were exceptions: Black Bart neither drank, smoked nor swore. Neither did Henry Starr, who added caffeine to his abstinence list: "I had determined to always keep a clear head, so if shooting occurred I could give a good account of myself." And it's noteworthy that both of these Bad Men had quite long and successful careers outside the law.

Cole Younger claimed, "for all my faults, and I am sorry to say there are many, whiskey drinking was not one of them and I never had confidence in a man who drank." In fact, Cole, in his last years, admitted one of the problems at Northfield was, unknown to him, the three who went into the bank (Jesse, Frank & Bob Y.) had consumed a quart of whiskey, clouding their judgement (and no doubt affecting the bank employees attitude towards them: "we've got three drunks in here, reeking of liquor, we can outsmart them"— which they did).

Legion are the Bad Men who were described as "genial and intelligent when sober, but uncontrollable when drunk." Famous names who staggered under the influence included Buckskin Frank Leslie, Johnny Ringo, Jack Slade, Curly Bill Brocius, Grat Dalton, John Wesley Hardin, Clay Allison, and, of course, Doc Holliday.

While most frontier towns had their fair share of drinking establishments, Tombstone allegedly had some 66 saloons supported by a population of between five and eight thousand. Considering that a large proportion of the populace was armed and drinking, it's incredible that there weren't more killings.

In fact, it's probably safe to say, if liquor had been taken out of the Old West equation this would be a very short book!

THE WIND & THE LION
As a longtime bartender in many a boomtown, Wyatt Earp no doubt endured his share of windy braggarts. (BBB)

enforcement officials now feel they have turned the corner on bringing down the James boys once and for all.

January 26, 1882
The stagecoach from Ukiah to Cloverdale, California, is robbed by Black Bart.

March 18, 1882
While shooting pool at Campbell and Hatch's Saloon in Tombstone, Morgan Earp is shot and killed by assailants shooting through the upper window in the rear door. Brother Wyatt Earp narrowly misses being shot also as a second bullet thuds above his head.

March 20, 1882
Cow-boy, stage robber and former deputy sheriff, Frank Stilwell, believed to be one of the men responsible for Morgan Earp's death, is shot dead at the train station at Tucson. His body is found the next morning riddled with bullets and buckshot. An indictment for murder is issued for Doc Holliday, Wyatt Earp, Warren Earp, Sherman McMasters and John "Turkey Creek" Johnson.

March 22, 1882
During his so-called Vendetta Ride, Wyatt Earp and cohorts shoot and kill Florentino Cruz. [And, according to Wyatt Earp, he kills Curly Bill the next day, at Mescal Springs.]

March 26, 1882
Two masked men rob the Tombstone Mill & Mining Co., killing M.R. Peel. [A posse led by Deputy Billy Breakenridge shoots it out with the two suspects, Billy Grounds and Zwing Hunt. Grounds is killed and Hunt captured.]

April 3, 1882

Zerelda James becomes a widow when her husband, "Thomas Howard," is shot and killed as he straightens a picture on a wall of their rented home in Saint Joseph, Missouri (see sidebar).

April 13, 1882

Oscar Wilde lectures at the Tabor Opera House in Denver. Admission is $1.50.

April 16, 1882

Five outlaws wreck an Atchison, Topeka and Santa Fe train at Rincon, N.M., killing the engineer and fireman. The raiders mistake the baggage car for the express car and before they can gain entry are run off by angry passengers.

Rincon Station, N.M., 1892 (MNM)

April 20, 1882

Sam and Belle Starr are arrested at Younger's Bend, Oklahoma, for stealing horses.

May 6, 1882

His veto overridden, President Arthur signs the Chinese Exclusion Act into law. It will halt labor immigration from China for ten years.

May 15, 1882

Doc Holliday is arrested at Denver, Colorado, by a con man claiming to be an officer.

June 14, 1882

Three miles from Little Lake, California, Black Bart robs the stage.

(BBB)

JESSE JAMES.

At 2 o'clock To-Day,

MONDAY, APRIL 10

—THE—

Household Goods

And all the Effects of the late

JESSE JAMES

WILL BE SOLD

AT AUCTION,

Upon the premises occupied by him,

Cor. 13th and Lafayette.

The proceeds are for the benefit of the widow and children, who are in need.

N. B.—There will be for sale, among other things, 1 Gold Watch, 1 small Revolver, Valise, and other articles owned and carried by the late Jesse James.

R. J. HAIRE,

Geo. P. Dilson
Auctioneer

Attorney for MRS. JAMES.
1882

JESSE DEPARTS

After Jesse was shot by Bob Ford, the outlaw leader's body was taken to the undertaker and a photo was taken (above). Note exit bullet wound near left eye. As to Jesse's command of his outlaw kingdom, slayer Bob Ford scoffed: "Jesse had outlived his greatness as a bandit...As a leader he was dead. There were but few who would place themselves in his clutches. Even his brother, Frank, kept continually hundreds of miles away...It was his tyranny among his fellows that wrecked his empire." An auction was held of Jesse's belongings and it all went for less than $200. (PHOTO, BOB McCUBBIN COLLECTION; POSTER, LEE POLLOCK)

Johnny Ringo:
Hails from Indiana, is a crack shot and crony of Curly Bill and Pony Diehl. Allegedly broke jail in Texas several times, shot a man in Safford, A.T., over a drink, gravitates between Galeyville and Tombstone.

Description:
Slim, 5' 11", fair, with brown hair and blue eyes, quiet-spoken and genial when sober, but apt to be moody and morose when drunk.

Alias:
Dutch John

Real Name:
John Peters Ringo

Johnny Ringo (JACK BURROWS)

HONOR AMONG THE MEN OF THE ROAD

In 1882, a writer coming in on the Tombstone stage related this encounter with the driver: "A guard got up with a Winchester rifle, and posted himself by the Wells Fargo box, and the driver began almost at once to relate robber stories. His stage had been stopped and 'gone through' twice within the past six months. The affair had been enlivened on the one occasion by a runaway and turnover, and on the other by the shooting and killing of the driver. Of this last item his successor spoke with natural disgust. If the line could not be drawn at drivers, he said, things had indeed come to a pretty pass. He respected a man who took to the road and robbed those who could afford it. At least, he considered it more honorable than borrowing money of a friend which you knew you would never repay." (BBB)

A TYPICAL "MUD WAGON" STAGE THAT SERVICED TOMBSTONE AND THE WEST. (AC)

June 17, 1882
A tornado devastates 200 miles of Iowa, killing 130.

June 24, 1882
Nat Greer and a party of Texas cow-boys stage a wild street battle with the Mexican population of St. Johns, Arizona. Two are killed.

July 11, 1882
Ben Thompson kills Jack Harris at San Antonio, Texas.

July 13, 1882
Black Bart is foiled when he attempts to rob the Laporte to Oroville stage. Two blasts from the messenger's sawed-off shotgun sends the outlaw scurrying away, empty-handed. [A buckshot pellet creases the robber's forehead, leaving a deep scar.]

July 14, 1882
In southeastern Arizona, the body of John Ringo is found in the bough of a tree in Turkey Creek Canyon. He had removed his boots and his swollen feet were wrapped in his undershirt and his pistol was caught in his watch chain [although several men take credit for his death, the official autopsy lists his death as a suicide].

July 22, 1882
United States Marshal Crawley Dake resigns. [He will be sued by the government for some $50,000 in missing funds. Of this, approximately $3,000 was money he gave to Wyatt Earp to pursue cow-boys in March. Earp is contacted in Colorado about the money and he claims Dake took him aside and confessed to drinking quite a bit of wine. The money is never repaid.]

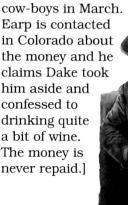

(BBB)

July 23, 1882

At Globe City, Arizona, citizens hang two killers from a tree.

July 26, 1882

Judge Roy Bean opens a saloon at Eagle's Nest Springs, Texas and begins to sit in judgement. [Even though he will not be officially a magistrate until December.]

September 11, 1882

In Bisbee, Arizona, miners halt work to lynch a drunken killer.

September 17, 1882

The stage from Yreka to Redding, California, is robbed by Black Bart.

September 18, 1882

The Manning brothers kill Dallas Stoudenmire at El Paso, Texas.

October 5, 1882

Frank James surrenders to Governor Crittendon at Jefferson City, Missouri.

November 14, 1882

Buckskin Frank Leslie shoots and kills Billy Claiborne outside the Oriental Saloon in Tombstone.

November 24, 1882

Six miles from Cloverdale, California, Black Bart robs the stage.

1883

The Supreme Court rules that Indians are "aliens" and dependents of the U.S. government. Miram Maxim invents the machine gun.

January 22, 1883

In Nevada, Wells Fargo messenger, Aaron "Hold-the Fort" Ross, becomes a hero when he survives repeated attempts by five outlaws trying to get into the express car he is guarding.

BUCKSKIN FRANK LESLIE SHOOTS AND KILLS BILLY CLAIBORNE

BUCKSKIN FRANK LESLIE
As he appeared in Tombstone.

—*George Parsons' Journal entry for Tuesday, November 14, 1882* "[Buckskin Frank Leslie] shot and killed the notorious Kid Claiborne this a.m. at 7:30, making as pretty a center shot on the Kid as one could wish to. The Kid threatened and laid for him near the Oriental with a Winchester, but Frank got the drop on him, being quick as lightning and used to killing men, and the Kid has gone to Hell. I say so because, if such a place exists and is for bad men, he is there, as he was a notoriously bad egg and has innocent blood on his head. I state facts...Frank didn't lose the light of his cigarette during the encounter. Wonderfully cool man." (BOTH ILLUSTRATIONS, BBB)

DODGE CITY PEACE COMMISSION

Photo taken in 1883 when Wyatt Earp (seated, second from left) *and Bat Masterson* (standing, at left) *came to Dodge City to support Luke Short* (standing, second from left) *in his feud with the mayor.* (PHOTO COURTESY OF JEFF MOREY)

LAW WEST OF THE PECOS

Roy Bean (the same Bad Man who fought duels in San Diego and Los Angeles, see 1852 entries) now declares himself a judge and opens up The Jersey Lilly in Vinegaroon, Texas. There he dispenses his own unique brand of justice (a lawyer told Bean he intended to habeas corpus his client and the judge threatened to hang the attorney for using profanity in his court). In the famous photo below, we see Judge Roy Bean on the porch, while his mounted deputies stand by.
(BOTH PHOTOS, BOB MCCUBBIN COLLECTION)

March 17, 1883
The Maricopa and Prescott mail stage is held up near Bumble Bee station, Arizona, and the Wells Fargo box taken.

April 12, 1883
Five miles from Cloverdale, California, the stage is robbed by Black Bart.

May 1, 1883
In Omaha, Buffalo Bill stages his first "Wild West" show.

June 5, 1883
Wyatt Earp, Bat Masterson, Charlie Bassett and others arrive in Dodge City to support Luke Short in his differences with the mayor. While in town they sit for their famous "Peace Commission" photo (see photo).

June 23, 1883
Four miles from Jackson, California, Black Bart robs the stage.

June 27, 1883
In central Arizona, the Black Canyon stage is robbed.

July 1, 1883
The Black Canyon stage is robbed again.

July 10, 1883
Between Florence and Globe, Arizona, Joe Tuttle and Len Redfield rob a stagecoach, killing the guard, John Collins. [A vigilante posse catches the outlaws and they are hung on Sept. 3rd.]

July 21, 1883
Two of the Black Canyon stage robbers are caught. One turns out to be the village blacksmith at nearby Gillett, Arizona.

August 12, 1883
Two Arizona stages are robbed on the same night. The Florence-Globe stage and the Prescott-Ashfork line. The Wells Fargo messenger on the Florence run is killed.

September 12, 1883

Soccoro, N.M., rancher and Bad Man, Joe Fowler, kills a man.

October 4, 1883

Two of the Globe-Florence stage robbers are killed in a gun battle with sheriff and posse.

November 3, 1883

Three miles from Copperopolis, California, Black Bart robs the Sonora and Milton stage on Funk Hill (the site of the very first Black Bart holdup in 1875). A young hunter on board the stage is carrying a Henry rifle and he snaps off a shot (after the stage driver fired twice with the weapon and failed to hit Bart). With the hunter's shot, the robber stumbles, dropping papers and then disappears (see sidebar).

November 6, 1883

Bad Man, Joe Fowler, kills Jim Cale while they are drinking at Soccoro, N.M. Fowler had just sold his ranch for a reported $53,500, and was celebrating. He is arrested and denied bail.

November 17, 1883

Black Bart pleads guilty to stage robbery at San Andreas, California and gets six years.

A Sample of Black Bart's Doggeral

Here I lay me down to sleep

To wait the coming morrow,

Perhaps success, perhaps defeat

And everlasting sorrow,

Yet come what will, I'll try it once,

My condition can't be worse,

And if there's money in that box,

'Tis munney in my purse.

*I've labored long and hard
for bread,*

For honor and for riches,

*But on my corns too long
you've tred,*

You fine-haired sons of bitches!

BLACK BART'S METHOD

Bart's robbery routine seldom varied. He invariably chose a spot near the top of a steep grade where a tired team had slowed to a walk. He would step directly into the road, brandishing a doubled-barreled shotgun and wearing a linen duster and a flour sack over his head with narrow slits for eyeholes. "Throw down the box!" was his terse, but efficient command. (WELLS FARGO BANK)

Black Bart: Terror of the Northern California stage line.

Description: He is about 5' 8" in height, straight as an arrow, broad shouldered, with deep sunken, bright blue eyes, high cheek bones, and a large, handsome grey mustache and imperial. According to detective Morse, "he looked anything but a stage robber."

Aliases: Black Bart C.E. Bolton

Real Name: Charles E. Boles

When his photo was taken at Stockton, Black Bart quipped: "Will that thing go off? I would like to go off myself."

(BBB)

BLACK BART: ONE SLIPPERY BAD MAN

Lawmen converged on the Funk Hill robbery site and completed a thorough search of the area, finding a hat, three pairs of cuffs, an opera glass case and a silk crepe handkerchief with the mark "F.X.O.7" on it.

Believing the notorious bandit to be from the San Francisco area, detective Harry Morse began a systematic search of the 91 laundries in the city. After numerous dead ends, Morse finally found "the identical mark" at a laundry at 316 Bush Street. From the laundryman, Morse learned the owner of the handkerchief was a mining man named C.E. Bolton. He also learned that Bolton roomed at No. 37 Second Street, room 40.

Two hours later, the suspect came walking into the laundry. The owner introduced Bolton to Morse, who later described his prey: "He was elegantly dressed and came sauntering along carrying a little cane. He wore a natty little derby hat, a diamond pin, a large diamond ring on his little finger, and a heavy gold watch and chain."

Using an assumed name, Morse talked Bolton into going for a walk to talk about his mines. As they walked and chatted, Morse steered Bolton into the Wells Fargo offices, where the detective took the still unsuspecting Bad Man up to the superintendent's office. There, Mr. Jim Hume and Morse grilled the outlaw for three hours until "great drops of perspiration stood out on his forehead and nose." The lawmen accompanied Bolton (still maintaining his innocence) to his residence where they gathered more evidence against him, including more laundry marks matching the robbery site linen and letters containing Bolton's handwriting which matched the doggerel poems left at prior robbery sites.

Charles E. Boles, a.k.a. C.E. Bolton and Black Bart, was put in jail that night and then taken by rail to Stockton, where he was positively I.D.'d by several eye witnesses. Hundreds lined the streets to see the famous robber and many mistook the nattily dressed outlaw for an officer and one of the policemen for the criminal.

Finally, Black Bart came clean to his captors and admitted his guilt. Morse recalled, "it was a great relief to him, for there had been a great strain on his mind, and this was the first time he had had the opportunity to tell anybody about this thing." Black Bart then led the officers to a hollow log where about $4,000 in gold amalgam was recovered.

On November 17, 1883, Black Bart pled guilty to a single charge of robbery, and was sentenced to a term of six years in San Quentin (he was a model prisoner and was released in four).

It wasn't long before the slippery stage robber was back on the front pages. After three stage holdups in July and November of 1888, Wells Fargo announced that Black Bart was, once again, the prime suspect. Then, with every lawman in northern California looking for him, Bart vanished into thin air. No one, including his wife and family, ever heard from him again.

Most Persistent Myth:

That Wells Fargo finally paid him a pension of $200 a month to leave their vehicles alone.

The Bertillon Method

In 1883, a Frenchman, Alphonse Bertillon, discovered there are 12 measurements on the human body which do not change in an adult: height, head length, outer arms, trunk, middle finger, forearm, etc. With these records, plus distinctive scars and markings, law enforcement have a "leg up" in collaring Bad Men. The Pinkertons begin using the Bertillon method in 1886.

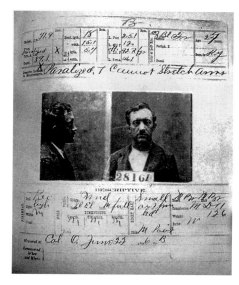

NAILED

Outlaw William Raidler's vital measurements are shown in his 1896 rap sheet. (GUTHRIE MUSEUM)

ISOM DART

A black cow-boy rustler from Colorado, who was assassinated by a hired gunman going by the name James Hicks, who turned out to be Tom Horn. (BBB)

FAMOUS LAST WORDS

Some effused poignantly, a few were quite profound, still others seemed confused or angry, but none of them whined.

• **Sam Bass:** "Let me go. The world is bobbing around..."

• **Doc Holliday:** "This is funny."

• **Billy the Kid:** "Quien es?" ("Who is it?")

• **Morgan Earp:** "This is the last game of pool I'll ever play."

• **Billy Clanton:** "They've murdered me!"

• **Bob Dalton:** "Die game!"

• **Pancho Villa:** "Don't let it end like this. Tell them I said something important."

• **Bill Brazelton:** "You Son of a Bitch!"

• **Charlie Bowdre:** "I wish...I wish..."

• **John Wesley Hardin:** "You have four sixes to beat."

• **Wild Bill Longley** (hung): "I see a good many enemies around, and mighty few friends."

• **Chacon** (hung): "Adios, todos amigos!" (Goodbye, all my friends!")

• **Blackjack Ketchum** (hung): "I'll be in Hell before you start breakfast, boys. Let 'er go!"

• **Henry Plummer** (hung): "Give me a good drop."

• **Wyatt Earp:** "Suppose...Suppose..."

KNOCKIN' ON HEAVEN'S DOOR

Most outlaws and Bad Men were knocking on a lower door and knew it (see several of the hanging quotes at left). *There is a breathtaking acceptance of responsibility for their actions that seems to be missing in a later age.*
(DENVER PUBLIC LIBRARY, WESTERN HISTORY DEPARTMENT)

Joel Fowler: Slightly built, dark brown eyes and hair, 5' 4", and weighs 130 pounds.

Aliases: None

Comments: Decent actor

JOEL FOWLER, 1882

Hailing from Massachusetts, Joel A. Fowler (above) gave his profession as "variety-actor." He allegedly studied law in Fort Worth, Texas, but after killing a man, moved to Las Vegas, N.M., where he became involved in a saloon and theatre. He acted in some of the plays, but alcohol was a problem. After a stint in White Oaks, Fowler took up ranching near Socorro, N.M., and there he killed two men while on a spree. Tired of his shenanigans, the vigilantes took him from jail and strung him up. Witnesses said Fowler began calling on "heavenly angels," prompting a member of the mob to retort: "It's a cold night for angels, Joel. Better call on someone nearer town." (JOSEPH P. SMITH PHOTO, UNM)

BISBEE MASSACRE

A gang of five "cow-boys" killed four people as they rode out of Bisbee, A.T. They would pay dearly for their deed.
(BBB)

HANGING HEATH

A mob came up from Bisbee and lynched John Heath from a Tombstone telegraph pole for his part in the Bisbee Massacre.
(TOMBSTONE COURTHOUSE STATE HISTORIC PARK)

November 18, 1883
The United States adopts Standard Time, dividing the nation into four time zones: Eastern, Central, Mountain and Pacific.

December 8, 1883
Five so-called cow-boys rob the Goldwater and Castenada Store at Bisbee, Arizona and shoot up the town killing four citizens in the process. It becomes known as the Bisbee Massacre.

1884

The song "Rock-a-bye Baby" is a hit.

January 13, 1884
The Black Canyon stage is robbed near Gillett, Arizona.

January 20, 1884
The Wickenburg stage is robbed near Prescott, Arizona.

January 22, 1884
Joel Fowler is lynched at Soccoro, N.M., for the killing of Jim Cale.

February 22, 1884
John Heath is lynched at Tombstone for his part in the Bisbee Massacre.

March 10, 1884
Four train robbers and a killer under a death sentence escape from the Silver City, N.M., jail. The escapees are caught three miles north of town and after a running gun battle, two of the outlaws are killed, two are captured and later lynched.

March 11, 1884
Ben Thompson and King Fisher are shot dead in San Antonio, Texas.

March 27, 1884
The first long-distance telephone call is made between Boston and New York City.

March 28, 1884

Convicted of murder for the Bisbee Massacre, five bandits are hanged simultaneously at Tombstone from the same gallows.

April 21, 1884

The Black Canyon stage is held up near Soap Springs, Arizona.

May 1, 1884

In Chicago, construction begins on a ten-story office building at the corner of LaSalle and Adams. It will be the first building to be called a "skyscraper."

June 1, 1884

The Black Canyon stage is held up again and robbed.

July 1, 1884

Buffalo are nearly extinct with an estimated 1,100 remaining in the United States and Canada.

July 8, 1884

Montana vigilantes trail and launch an attack against a group of 10 known rustlers. In the shootout at Bates Point, 15 miles below the mouth of Musselshell River, Montana, five of the outlaws are killed, four are captured and one escapes. The next day at the mouth of Musselshell River, the vigilantes hang Dixie Burr, Silas Nickerson, Swift Bill and Orville Edwards.

August 19, 1884

Doc Holliday shoots Billy Allen in the right arm at Leadville, Colorado.

October 18, 1884

Arizona outlaws rob travelers on the Black Canyon road and then wait for the stage and hold it up—again.

November, 1884

Wells Fargo reports that between November 1870 and November 1884 there have been 313 stage robberies and 34 attempted robberies with a

A FEARLESS BUGGER

Known as a "four-eyed" dude, Dakota rancher, Teddy Roosevelt, (above center) was an object of curiosity in the Badlands. But as a freak winter storm buried the surrounding area in March of 1886 Roosevelt was about to win a new appellation.

Early on the morning of March 24, a ranch hand went out onto the piazza and found Roosevelt's scow gone. It had been cut loose with a knife. Nearby, at the edge of the water, the men found a red woolen mitten. Roosevelt was so angry he wanted to chase the thieves on horseback but was dissuaded by his employees.

Roosevelt sent to Medora for a bag of nails and his men began to build a second keelboat. It didn't take much detective work to figure out who the robbers were: three "hard characters who lived in a shack, or hut, some twenty miles above us, and whom we had shrewdly suspected for some time of wishing to get out of the

TR's Two Armed Ranch Hands Ready to Ride (in a Boat).

country, as certain of the cattlemen had begun openly to threaten to lynch them."

Under arctic conditions, Teddy, along with two ranch hands, went after the thieves in a hastily built second boat. Nearly 100 miles downstream, the intrepid posse rounded a bend and almost collided with the stolen boat.

Without hesitation, Teddy jumped ashore and peered into the outlaw's camp. After mooring their boat, the three men pounced on the hapless cook, then waited for the other two to come in from hunting. Within the hour, all three were captured without incident.

Most Westerners would have executed the thieves on the spot, but Roosevelt insisted on personally remanding the prisoners to jail. After taking their photographs (Teddy brought a camera!), the men and their prisoners steered the two boats through the ice flows, and in between guard duty, Teddy read *Anna Karenina*, later remarking, "My surroundings were quite grey enough to harmonize with Tolstoy."

On April 7, Teddy sent his men on downriver with the boats, while he and his prisoners trekked overland in the snow and mud, 45 miles to the nearest jail.

With blisters on his feet, and travelling without sleep for 36 hours, Deputy Roosevelt singlehandedly turned over his prisoners to the sheriff at Dickerson, Dakota and received his duly earned fees as a deputy sheriff—$50.

When word of the capture spread across the West, Roosevelt became something of a folk hero and instead of "Four Eyes," his neighbors bestowed upon him a new nickname: "A fearless bugger."

DEPUTY SHERIFF ROOSEVELT
"We took them absolutely by surprise," Teddy remarked. Here are two photos of Roosevelt's prisoners, Burnsted (the half-breed), Pfaffenbach (a half-wit) and "Redhead" Finnegan, a long-haired gunman of vicious reputation.
(ALL PHOTOS, THEODORE ROOSEVELT ASSOCIATION)

loss of $415,312. Sixteen drivers and guards have been shot to death, seven outlaws hanged by mobs and 16 killed in gun battles and 240 robbers were convicted and imprisoned.

March 5, 1885
Karl Benz of Germany builds the first internal combustion automobile.

February 4, 1886
Outlaw Dennis Dilda is hanged for murder in Prescott, Arizona, but not before he ate his last meal. At his request he ordered "breaded spring chicken, cream sauce, fried oysters, lamb chops, green peas, tenderloin steak with mushrooms, English pancake with jelly, potatoes, bread and coffee." No record of whether he asked for seconds.

July 16, 1886
Ned Buntline, real name Edward Zane Carroll Judson, dies in New York. Buntline was the king of the dime novels and author of the *Scouts of the Plains* which launched Buffalo Bill's fame.

October 25, 1886
Six masked men hold up the St. Louis and San Francisco Railroad near Saint Louis, Missouri and get off with $57,000. [The messenger and another outlaw are arrested and convicted.]

October 28, 1886
The Statue of Liberty is dedicated on Bedloe's Island in New York Harbor.

December, 1886
Wells Fargo reports there were only 15 stage robberies for the year and the total amount taken was $300.

1887

The Dawes Act terminates tribal government and communal ownership of tribal lands.
The worst winter storm on record kills millions of cattle and bankrupts numerous ranchers throughout Montana, Wyoming, Kansas and the Dakotas.

January 19, 1887

A Flagstaff, Arizona mob breaks in the jail doors and kills two prisoners being held on a charge of murder.

January 23, 1887

The Burrow gang robs the Texas & Pacific Railroad at Gordon, Texas and gets off with about $4,500.

January 28, 1887

Two masked men rob a Southern Pacific passenger train, 17 miles east of Tucson, Arizona and get away with $20,000. This is the first recorded train robbery in Arizona.

March 15, 1887

An employee of the Triple V ranch rides into Sundance, Wyoming and reports the theft of a six-shooter, a horse, saddle, bridle and chaps. The thief is reported to be "a smooth-faced, grey-eyed boy" named Harry Longabaugh [soon to become known as, "The Sundance Kid"].

July 1, 1887

Feared killer, Clay Allison is himself murdered near Pecos, Texas, when a wagon wheel passes over his head. It has never been clearly determined how it happened.

August 5, 1887

In Wyoming, Harry "Sundance Kid" Longabaugh is sentenced to 18 months hard labor for horse stealing.

ONE SMALL STRIDE FOR WESTERNS

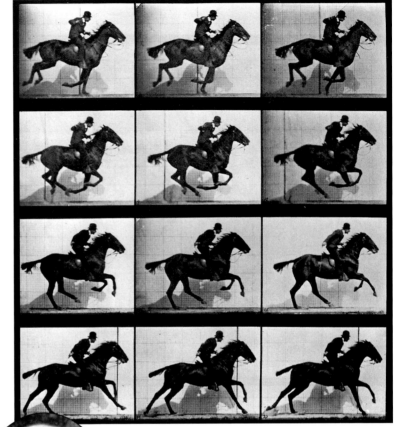

In 1872, California railroad magnate and horse breeder, Leland Standford, believed that when a horse is running, at some point, the horse will have all four legs off the ground simultaneously. He made a $25,000 wager with a friend and then tried to get photographer Eadward Muybridge (at left) to help him prove it.

Muybridge was intrigued and challenged by the proposition because up to that time no photographs had been taken at the speeds necessary to capture such action. But before he could act, a personal tragedy almost ended his career.

The photographer discovered the son borne to him by his younger wife was not his. Having determined the real father to be one Harry Larkyns, Muybridge sought out the man and shot him to death. A lynch mob almost hung him, but he escaped that fate and at his trial in 1875, he was acquitted on the grounds that Larkyns had deserved his fate.

Muybridge resumed his collaboration with Stanford and developed chemical and mechanical techniques to capture motion sequences. Stanford won his bet and Muybridge became world famous for his series of "motion pictures." The above images were captured at Gentleman's Driving Park in 1885. (ALL PHOTOS, EADWARD MUYBRIDGE PHOTOS)

COMMODORE PERRY OWENS

From Tennessee, Owens migrated to New Mexico, then settled at Navajo Springs, Arizona, in 1882. Said to be an excellent shot, he managed a stage station for a time, then turned his pursuits to law enforcement. Elected sheriff of Apache County in November of 1886, Owens had his famous shootout with the Blevins crowd at Holbrook, killing three and wounding a fourth, all with five shots. He was the first sheriff of Navajo County from 1895 to 1896. Around 1900 he went into business at Seligman, A.T. Owens was 5' 10", with grey eyes and blond hair, worn scout style. He is shown here wearing a "buscadero rig" (a holster style rarely seen in the Old West and made popular in the 1950s). (BOB MCCUBBIN COLLECTION)

FLAGSTAFF, ARIZONA TERRITORY

The fledgling railroad town as it appeared at the time of the lynching (see Jan. 19, 1887). Of course, Flagstaff has a dubious distinction in the legend of moviemaking. It was here that Jesse Laskey and Cecil B. DeMille were bound for when they left the east in 1911 to find a place out west to make movies. Tradition says there was a snowstorm when they arrived and, taking one look out the window, they decided to ride the rails to the end of the line and see what they might find—Hollywood. (BEN WITTICK PHOTO)

August 9, 1887

In the first pitched battle of what will become known as the Pleasant Valley War, a shootout at the Tewksbury cabin ends with the death of two and the wounding of three others.

September 4, 1887

Sheriff Commodore Perry Owens shoots four (and kills three) members of the so-called Blevins Gang in Holbrook, Arizona.

September 20, 1887

The Burrow gang robs the Texas and Pacific train at the same spot as on June 4th and get away with $2,725.

November 3, 1887

Four outlaws rob the Denver and Rio Grande passenger train at Unaweep Switch, five miles east of Grand Junction, Colorado. [All four are eventually caught near Price, Utah.]

November 8, 1887

Doc Holliday dies at Glenwood Springs, Colorado. His last words are, "This is funny," referring to the fact that in spite of his constant effort to the contrary, he will die with his boots off.

December 9, 1887

The Burrow gang robs the Texas Pacific Railroad at Genoa, Arkansas and get off with about $2,000. [On Dec. 31, one of the robbers is arrested and implicates the Burrow brothers.]

1888

The Washington Monument
is completed.
Jack the Ripper terrorizes London.
"Casey at the Bat" is published.

March 19, 1888

The Atlantic and Pacific Express is robbed at Canyon Diablo, Arizona, by four outlaws. [The robbers are tracked down by a posse led by Sheriff Buckey O'Neill (see photo opposite page), and sent to prison.]

March 23, 1888

In the state of Chihuahua, Old Mexico, lawman Bob Paul, with the assistance of Mexican police, tracks down and kills three members of the Larry Sheehan gang, which had recently robbed two trains in Arizona.

July 3, 1888

Wyatt Earp's second wife (no record has been found of their marriage), Mattie Blaylock, commits suicide at Pinal, Arizona, from an overdose of laudanum at age 30.

July 4, 1888

Tom Horn wins first place in steer roping at Globe, Arizona.

August 15, 1888

Outlaws lynch three men in Holbrook, Arizona, in aftermath of the Pleasant Valley War.

November 15, 1888

Rube Burrow and two others rob the Illinois Central train. A passenger, Chester Hughes is killed. [Not long after, a Nashville conductor recognizes Jim and Rube Burrow and notifies police. Rube shoots his way clear, but Jim is captured and dies in prison.]

HOLBROOK, ARIZONA TERRITORY

A rough railroad town. (BEN WITTICK PHOTO)

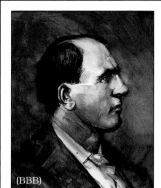

(BBB)

Tom Horn:
Cow-boy, scout and hired assassin.

Description:
6' 2", deep-chested, erect and of considerable strength. Light complexion with sandy hair and blue eyes.

Aliases:
James Hicks, Tom Hale

TOM HORN

A Missouri lad, Horn landed in Santa Fe and worked as a stage driver, then drifted into Arizona and became an Army "scrub packer" in 1882. He saw action in the Apache Wars and was with Gen. Crook on his 1883 Sierra Madre expedition. He later was named chief of scouts under Capt. Crawford and was with that officer in Sonora when he was killed by Mexican irregulars, Horn being wounded in the arm. After the surrender of Geronimo, in which he also had a hand, Horn was discharged and tried mining for a while, then became a cow-boy. Horn was an excellent roper (see July 4, 1888). He also claimed he was involved in the Pleasant Valley War and may have killed Old Man Blevins (based on his statement to Jo LeFors that he killed his first man when he was 26, adding, "he was a coarse S.O.B."). Somewhere in this time frame Horn decided to become a paid assassin.

(BBB)

PRESCOTT POSSE

Yavapai County Sheriff Buckey O'Neill (third from left) and the posse that tracked down the Bad Men (who turned out to be four bored cow-boys) who robbed an Atlantic & Pacific train at Diablo Canyon Station, Arizona. Joined by two railroad detectives, O'Neill and his posse picked up the trail and tracked the fugitives into Utah. After a gunfight near Wah Weep Canyon, in which O'Neill had his horse shot out from under him, the outlaws surrendered.
(SHARLOT HALL MUSEUM)

WHAM ROBBERY SITE

The above photo was taken 24 hours after the robbery. Note the dead mule still at the scene. This photo was obviously the photo reference for artist Frederick Remington's illustration (at right), of the infamous holdup.
(ARIZONA HISTORICAL SOCIETY)

January 19, 1889

At Graham, Texas, four of the outlaw Marlow Brothers are shackled together and transported by wagon to the railhead when the convoy is attacked by a mob at a creek crossing. A major battle ensues with heavy casualties on both sides: five dead and five wounded, including two of the Marlow brothers, Lep and Alf. Both of the surviving Marlows are wounded but they take weapons off the wounded and dying lawmen and help beat back the mob. They then, cut the feet off their dead brothers to facilitate their escape!

February 3, 1889

Texas outlaw, Belle Starr, is shot dead in Indian Territory, by persons unknown.

February 4, 1889

Harry Longabaugh is released from the Crook County jail after receiving a pardon from Gov. Moonlight. He takes the alias "Sundance Kid" and departs for parts unknown.

February 22, 1889

The Omnibus Bill is signed by President Cleveland, which admits Washington, Montana, North and South Dakota into the Union.

April 22, 1889

A pistol shot rings out at high noon and the Oklahoma Land Rush is on. Thousands of settlers swarm on 1.9 million acres in central Oklahoma trying to make a claim on the best land.

May 11, 1889

The U.S. army paymaster wagon is attacked near Cedar Springs, Arizona and $26,000 is taken. This becomes known as the "Wham Robbery," named after the paymaster, Major J.W. Wham. [Five local ranchers are tried for the crime in federal court, but are acquitted, partly because of local animosity for the federal government.]

July 10, 1889

In Tombstone, Arizona, Buckskin Frank Leslie kills his girlfriend, Mollie Williams while drunk. He tries to kill a witness, but Jim Neal escapes in the bushes. Frank pleads self-defense, but Neal's testimony convicts Leslie and he is sentenced to 25 years in Yuma Territorial Prison. [He is pardoned in 1897 and it is thought he went to Alaska.]

July 20, 1889

In Wyoming, Ella Watson, also known as "Cattle Kate," is lynched, along with James Averell near Independence Rock.

July 24, 1889

Butch Cassidy and others (accounts vary from two to five) rob the San Miguel Valley bank in Telluride, Colorado.

September 16, 1889

In Stillwater Prison, Bob Younger dies of tuberculosis.

November 2, 1889

The Apache Kid and five others kill their guards and escape while enroute to the Yuma Prison.

1890

*The U.S. Army battles Miniconjou Sioux at Wounded Knee.
62 Sioux women and children are killed.
The number of phone subscribers has reached 250,000 in the United States.*

January 10, 1890

Six men are hung at Fort Smith, Arkansas, for murders committed in the Indian Nations.

October 7, 1890

Rube Burrow is captured at Blue Lick, Alabama and taken to the county jail. [The next day he attempts to escape and is shot dead.]

(ARIZONA HISTORICAL SOCIETY)

Apache Kid:
Former sergeant under Chief of Scouts Al Sieber. Abused his rank by hunting down and killing several Apaches he blamed for his father's death. Spent a short time at Alcatraz, was retried and sentenced to seven years at Yuma. Escaped by killing his guards and currently is at large.

Description:
Medium height, athletic build, black hair and eyes, piercing stare.

Aliases:
Ski-be-nan-ted (sometimes spelled haskay-bay-nay-tay). Zenogalache (The Crazy One).

THE APACHE KID

Early in his life he came under the wing of Al Sieber, the noted army Chief of Scouts. A bright boy, he quickly rose through the ranks to first sergeant and he took part in the last Indian uprising in Arizona at the battle of Big Dry Wash, in July of 1882. In 1887, the Apache Kid was left in charge of the scouts and guardhouse at San Carlos while Al Sieber was away on business. During this time, the Kid's father was slain in a tiswin affair (tiswin being an Apache homemade alcoholic drink). Although the murderer of his father was also slain, the Kid used the incident and his authority to track down another Apache who the Kid suspected was behind the killing. After killing the suspect, the Kid returned and attempted to surrender to Sieber. The Kid was disarmed, but in the confusion that followed one of the Apache scouts fired his weapon and Sieber was shot in the left foot, permanently crippling him. The Kid and his band escaped and made their way towards Mexico, but the Kid had a change of heart and surrendered. Sentenced to seven years in the Yuma Territorial Prison, the Kid and other Apaches were being transferred from Globe to the railroad at Casa Grande, when the Kid, with others, overpowered his guards (see November 2, 1889). All the prisoners escaped and a posse sent out to track them down was stymied by a snowstorm which obliterated all their tracks. From that point on, the Apache Kid became a slippery ghost. Sightings of him were reported for years and his alleged raids became so widespread the Territorial legislature offered a $5,000 reward for him dead or alive. Several army officers were given roving commissions to track him down: all failed. (BBB)

Rube Burrow:

A farm boy from Alabama, Reuben (Rube) Houston Burrow and his brother Jim, took up rustling in the Oklahoma area (then known as Indian Territory). The Burrows quickly graduated to trains, and after a series of successful robberies in Texas, the Pinkertons were hot on their trail. During a train holdup in January, 1888, Jim Burrow was caught but Rube shot his way free. Nine months later, Jim died in jail from a fever. Soon, the rewards for Rube, dead or alive, totalled $7,500. The end came in October, 1890 after Rube was captured and attempted to escape. He managed to produce a weapon but died in an exchange of shots with lawman J.D. Carter.

Unusual Abilities:

Legend says he could hit a woodknot with a rifle at 100 yards.

Aliases:

The Mail-Clad Desperado (Rube was alleged to wear a chain-mail vest).

(AC)

November 4, 1890

Outlaw Marian Hegepeth and his gang rob the Missouri Pacific Railroad near Omaha, Nebraska, getting away with about $1,000.

February 6, 1891

The Dalton gang attempts to rob a southbound Southern Pacific passenger train near Alila, California. A fireman is killed and the gang gets away with no loot.

April 7, 1891

The Nebraska legislature enacts a statute providing for an eight-hour work day.

May 9, 1891

The Dalton gang robs the Santa Fe Railroad at Wharton (Perry), Oklahoma.

September 15, 1891

The Dalton gang robs the Missouri, Kansas and Texas Railroad at Lillietta, Oklahoma.

November (c), 1891

At the Arizona Territorial Fair in Phoenix, Tom Horn sets a world record for steer roping, beating his archrival "Arizona Charlie" Meadows. Horn's record of 49 and a half seconds is a marvel of its day.

1892

*The Johnson County War in Wyoming ignites.
Vogue magazine is launched.*

March 1, 1892

Thomas Edison completes the first moving picture studio at West Orange, New Jersey. He pays $637.37 for the building.

April 8, 1892

In Wyoming, Robert Parker, alias "Butch Cassidy," is arrested for horse theft.

THE INFAMOUS DUNN BROTHERS

Working both sides of the law, the Dunn brothers were rough customers. Bee sold out his outlaw pals, Bitter Creek Newcomb and Charley Pierce by filling them with buckshot to claim the reward. The Dunns also worked with Heck Thomas on the side of the law. (UNIVERSITY OF OKLAHOMA)

April 9, 1892

Nate Champion and Nick Ray are killed at the KC ranch in Wyoming.

June 1, 1892

The Daltons rob the Santa Fe Railroad at Red Rock Station, Oklahoma.

June 8, 1892

Ed Kelly shoots and kills Bob Ford with a shotgun in Ford's tent saloon in Creede, Colorado. Bob had accused Kelly of stealing a diamond ring.

July, 1892

Henry Starr and two others rob the Nowata, Oklahoma, train station of $1,700. [Starr is arrested the next day but jumps bond.]

July 14, 1892

The Dalton gang robs the Missouri, Kansas & Texas railroad at Adair, Oklahoma. As the outlaws attack the train at the station, three lawmen and a railroad guard open fire on them from a shed near the tracks. While part of the gang holds off the men in the shed, three of the outlaws work their way around to the opposite side of the train, away from the lawmen's guns. Forcing their way into the express car, they quickly blow the safe and grab the contents (although never verified, it is reported to be about $40,000). Stray bullets shatter the window of the town drugstore, where two doctors are sitting at a table. Both are injured and one of them, Dr. W.L. Goff, dies. All four of the guards in the shed are wounded and the outlaws escape.

July 23, 1892

Congress bans all liquor sales on Indian lands.

BOB DALTON
Bob had served previously as a deputy U.S. marshal. He was the leader of the ill-fated Coffeyville raid. (TOP PHOTOS, BOB McCUBBIN COLLECTION)

GRAT DALTON
Also a former deputy U.S. marshal, Grat was arrested and convicted for an Alila, California, train robbery in 1891, but escaped.

THE CONDON BANK IN COFFEYVILLE
One of the two targets the Daltons attempted to raid (the other being the First National Bank, just to the right and across a half-street, less than fifty feet away).

The photo (below) shows the firepower directed at the bank from Isham's (see opposite page).
(BOTH BANK PHOTOS, KANSAS STATE HISTORICAL SOCIETY)

DEAD DALTONS

Bob Dalton had planned the Coffeyville raid to "best anything Jesse James ever did—rob two banks at once in broad daylight." He didn't quite make it. He is seen (at right with torn pants, cut for souvenirs), handcuffed in death with Grat. Both have been stripped of their hats, weapons and boots. The dead outlaws were then piled together near the jail in Death Alley (below) and then wagon slats were laid out on the ground and propped up on some hay and the bodies laid upon it for the final series of photos (bottom).
(ALL PHOTOS THIS PAGE, KANSAS STATE HISTORICAL SOCIETY)

Four Fatal Mistakes

1. The Daltons' disguises (false whiskers) didn't work; townspeople recognized them immediately.
2. The street where the gang wanted to hitch their horses was torn up, so they reined up by the jail in an alley that looks directly into the front doors of Isham's Hardware Store.
3. Grat got stalled in the Condon bank too long.
4. The employees of Isham's Hardware Store handed out rifles and ammunition to volunteers, who took up well-guarded positions which covered the Condon Bank and the gang's retreat. And when the gang tried to make a run for it, the shooters in Isham's were literally shooting fish in a barrel.

September 13, 1892
Wanted for six train robberies, Chris Evans and John Sontag, ambush a posse in California's Sierra Nevada Mountains and kill two lawmen.

October 5, 1892
The Dalton gang tries unsuccessfully to rob two banks in Coffeyville, Kansas (see sidebar).

November 1, 1892
The Bill Doolin gang robs the Ford County Bank in Spearville, Kansas.

November 2-3, 1892
Sixteen lawmen surround Ned Christie's hideout and, after 30 cannon shots, and six dynamite sticks, the tenacious outlaw is shot down as he attempts to escape.

November 8, 1892
Henry Starr and Milo Creekmore rob a store in Nowata, Oklahoma and get away with $180. Starr is also suspected of being in on a Wharton train robbery on the same day.

November 19, 1892
Starr and Creekmore rob another store and get $521.

December 13, 1892
Henry Starr kills Deputy Marshal Floyd Wilson and escapes. [He forms a new gang and within days robs three banks, two railroads and three stores.]

1893

The Columbian Exposition opens in Chicago. The average U.S. worker now earns $9.42 a week.

May 5, 1893
Wall Street stock prices take a beating and the market collapses on June 27. 600 banks close their doors and more than 15,000 businesses fail.

June 5, 1893

The Henry Starr gang robs the People's Bank at Bentonville, Arkansas and gets away with $11,001.53.

June 11, 1893

At Stone Corral in the Sierra Nevada foothills, lawmen ambush Chris Evans and John Sontag. Evans is wounded and Sontag killed.

July 1, 1893

Henry Starr and Kid Wilson are captured at Colorado Springs. [Sentenced to hang, Starr gets two new trials, is finally allowed to plead guilty to manslaughter and gets five years.]

September 1, 1893

Lawmen shoot it out with the Doolin gang at Ingalls, Oklahoma (see sidebar, page 94).

September 8, 1893

Luke Short dies of dropsy at Geuda Springs, Kansas.

January 7, 1894

At the Thomas Edison Studio in West Orange, New Jersey, comedian Fred Ott is filmed sneezing.

March 13, 1894

Bill Doolin and Bill Dalton rob the depot at Woodward, Oklahoma.

March 16, 1894

John Wesley Hardin is granted a full pardon by Texas Governor James Hogg. [Wes has served 16 years of a 25-year sentence.]

April 5, 1894

In El Paso, Texas, Bass Outlaw kills a Texas Ranger and then is shot and killed by John Selman.

May 19, 1894

A shotgun messenger kills a lone bandit near Angel's Camp. [This marks the last stage robber killed in California.]

"The odor of a large, poorly kept jail is worse than the odor in the animal section of a circus."
—HENRY STARR, DESCRIBING CONDITIONS AT THE FORT SMITH PRISON

HENRY STARR IN CAPTIVITY
(above): *Photo of the 20-year-old bank robber, taken at Fort Smith, Arkansas, following Starr's capture at Colorado Springs on July 3, 1893.*
(right): *Judge Issac Parker, The Hanging Judge.*
(ALL THREE PHOTOS FROM GLENN SHIRLEY COLLECTION)

THE FORT SMITH FEDERAL BUILDING AND BASEMENT JAIL

Henry Starr spent five years at Fort Smith pending appeals. Twice Judge Issac Parker (above, right) sentenced Starr to the gallows and both times his ruling was reversed by the United States Supreme Court.

When Starr was ushered into the Fort Smith prison, he recalled, "The rough attitude of the officials chilled my heart." He claimed the first thing they did was fine him 50 cents for "breaking into jail without consent of the inmates." He wrote he "could also hear the yells and curses of the 200 prisoners, who were allowed to scream as loud and as long as they desired." One of them yelled, "Fresh fish!" and the others laughed and yelled.

"I was assigned to a cell," he later wrote. "The bedclothes reeking with filth and covered with lice. I sat all night on a small box as far from the bed as I could get...I am not ashamed to confess that I wept hot tears—not of fear, but of outraged young manhood."

Once he settled in, Starr was a model prisoner, reading and writing articles for newspapers about the Indian Territory and the Five Civilized Tribes. In spite of his good standing, he wrote that the prison was "a good investment for the making of outlaws."

BILL DALTON

He was active in the California Democratic party (although he was never a state assemblyman as some have claimed). After he and his brothers held up a Tulare County train, Bill rode the outlaw trail until he was shot dead by Oklahoma lawman. He was eloquent, and had a good sense of humor. (BOB MCCUBBIN COLLECTION)

(BBB)

Outlaw Matt Warner,
of the Wild Bunch.

June 8, 1894
Outlaw Bill Dalton is killed while resisting arrest at Ardmore, Oklahoma.

July 15, 1894
Convicted of horse stealing, Butch Cassidy enters Wyoming State Prison.

April 3, 1895
The Bill Doolin gang robs the Rock Island Railroad at Dover, Oklahoma. In a shootout with a posse gang member, "Tulsa Jack" Blake, is killed.

May 2, 1895
To collect the reward money, John Dal and Bee Dunn shoot and kill outlaws Charley Pierce and Bitter Creek Newcomb.

July 10, 1895
Former Regulator and cohort of Billy the Kid, Jose Chavez y Chavez is arrested at a sheep ranch west of Soccoro, N.M. He was tracked down by Sheriff Holm Bursum, of Las Vegas, N.M. Chavez was a member of the SOBs (Society of Bandits) and is sentenced to a life term in prison. [In 1905 he helps deter a prison riot and is pardoned by the governor.]

August 1, 1895
After a shootout with lawmen, Ike Black is killed and Zip Wyatt wounded. [Wyatt is latter shot again and captured, dying on September 8, 1895]

August 19, 1895
At the bar of the Acme Saloon, John Wesley Hardin is killed by John Selman in El Paso, Texas.

PRISONER #1089
Former Billy the Kid gang member, Jose Chavez Y Chavez, was pardoned in 1909 by the governor of New Mexico. (NEW MEXICO STATE RECORDS CENTER AND ARCHIVES)

THE LAWYER
John Wesley Hardin as he appeared in El Paso during the final years of his life.
(JEFF MOREY)

GUNFIGHT AT INGALLS

It was a warm September Friday when three covered wagons approached the outlaw town of Ingalls, Oklahoma. Concealed inside and disguised as Boomers (the officers in one wagon tried to pass themselves off as hunters), were 13 federal officers plus 11 hand-picked Stillwater men "known to be good shots." They converged on the tiny hamlet, ready to round up the Doolin gang in one fell swoop.

As the wagons pulled into town from opposite directions, one of the wagon drivers asked a local lad the identity of a rider coming towards them up the main street. "That's Bitter Creek!" the boy replied and officer Dick Speed raised his Winchester and fired.

Newcomb reeled in the saddle (Speed's bullet "burst the magazine" of Bitter Creek's rifle and ricocheted into his arm and groin). As the outlaw turned his horse to flee, Speed stepped out in the street to kill him. The rifle blast brought Arkansas Tom from his bed on the top floor of the O.K. Hotel and he took in the situation at a glance and shot Speed twice, killing him.

The firing had begun before many of the federal officers had reached their positions. Consequently, the outlaws were able to make a bold escape. The raging gunfight left three officers dead, two innocent bystanders killed and two other citizens and an outlaw badly wounded. Only one Bad Man was captured and Arkansas Tom, the man responsible for four of the deaths was left behind in the O.K. Hotel.

IN THE HIVE
The gang was all there: Dynamite Dick, Tulsa Jack, Bill Dalton and Bill Doolin, were in Ransoms & Murrays Saloon (right) playing poker. Bitter Creek Newcomb was getting a shoe tightened on his horse at Wagner's blacksmith shop. Arkansas Tom was in bed at the O.K. Hotel. (GLENN SHIIRLEY)

THE H.F. PIERCE LIVERY
Bill Doolin made a break from the saloon to this stable. He was quickly followed by Bill Dalton, Dynamite Dick and Tulsa Jack. While Doolin and Dynamite Dick saddled the horses, Dalton and Tulsa Jack kept up a steady fuselage at the officers. As the four outlaws burst from the stable, two from the front, two from the rear, an officer shot Dalton's horse in the jaw and he spun around, ran another 75 yards and fell again. With bullets whizzing around his head, Dulton retrieved his wire cutters from his saddlebags, ran to the fence and let the gang through. Doolin picked up Dalton and they rode into a 10 foot gully. The officers could only see their hats "until they came out of the gully on the jump." Jim Masterson (brother of Bat) said, "I raised my sight to 500 yards, but I couldn't get 'em." (BBB)

O.K. COVER FIRE
Arkansas Tom kept up a deadly fire from the top floor of the small O.K. Hotel. He punched holes in the roof and generally kept the superior federal force ducking for cover at every turn. After a tense standoff, he finally surrendered on the condition he not be lynched. Against the wishes of several officers, the request was honored. (PHOTO, GLENN SHIIRLEY; ILLUSTRATION, BBB)

THE UNIVERSITY OF BAD MEN

UTAH STATE PENITENTIARY (SAVAGE PHOTO)

While the frontier interior suffered from a lack of jails, other, more established areas suffer an age old problem:

"At night the convicts are locked in their cells, which are in three buildings standing parallel to each other, about twenty feet distant from each other. The cells of two of these buildings are intended for a single convict. There are thirty-three in a tier, with three on each side and three high...Above these rooms there are a row of twenty-four cells on each side, with four convicts to each. These cells are about eight feet long, five wide and eight high. There are two bunks, one on each side, two berths to each bunk. These cells are suitable enough for two men, but for four the air is intolerable."

—Charles Mortimer, describing his confinement at San Quentin in the 1860s

"What I did not already know of criminal life I could easily learn [at San Quentin]. There were there some ten or fifteen of the most notorious highwaymen on the coast, all in consultation."
—CHARLES MORTIMER

BILL DOOLIN BEHIND BARS
But not for long. Doolin escapes jail in Guthrie, Oklahoma, with several others and makes his way back to the Ingalls area he knows so well. (BBB)

YUMA TERRITORIAL PRISON
Known widely as the "Hellhole" of Western prisons, Yuma Territorial Prison boasted 120 degree days and scorpion filled cells at night. Prisoners are seen here working on a wall (note the thickness). (AC)

SAN QUENTIN PRISON
The largest jail on the Western slope, San Quentin received its share of hardcases from all over California. Located just north of San Francisco, San Quentin was a notorious training ground for highwaymen. (BILL SECREST)

1896

The Klondike gold rush begins.
The U.S. Post Office begins
Rural Free Delivery.
Utah is admitted as the 45th state
on the condition Mormons give up
polygamous marriage.

January 15, 1896
Lawman Bill Tilghman captures Bill Doolin in a bath house at Eureka Springs, Arkansas.

January 19, 1896
Butch Cassidy is released from prison with a pardon.

April 5, 1896
George Scarborough shoots John Selman after an argument in the Wigwam Saloon. [Selman dies the next day.]

June 10, 1896
Sam and Tom Ketchum loot a store and post office at Liberty, New Mexico. [A posse follows, but the outlaws kill two of the posse members and escape.]

July 1, 1896
In Fort Smith, Arkansas, Rufus Buck, Lucky Davis, Louis Davis, Sam Sampson and Maoma July, are hanged as a quintet for the rape of a woman in the Creek Nation on August 5, 1895.

July 5, 1896
At Guthrie, Oklahoma, prisoners "Dynamite Dick Clifton" and Bill Doolin escape jail.

August 6, 1896
The High Five gang led by "Black Jack" Christian attempts to rob the International Bank at Nogales, Arizona. [A Tucson posse catches up with the gang at Skeleton Canyon on the Arizona-New Mexico line. One posse member is killed and the gang escapes into Mexico. See photo at right.]

Robert Leroy Parker:
Cow-boy, rustler, bank robber and highwayman. Served time in Wyoming State Prison penitentiary at Laramie for grand larceny, but was pardoned January 19, 1896. Very charming, always smiling. Plays harmonica.

Description:
Blue-gray eyes, 5' 9", flaxen hair, weighs 165 pounds. Two cut scars on back of head, small scar under left eye, small brown mole on left calf.

Aliases:
Butch Cassidy, George Cassidy, Ingerfield, Jim Lowe.

BUTCH CASSIDY
Photo taken upon his release from prison. (WYOMING ARCHIVES)

FLY POSSE
A photo of the posse who chased the Black Jack Christian gang after their failed bank robbery attempt at Nogales. The man in the center foreground is alleged to be Camillus S. Fly, Tombstone's famous photographer, although there is little provenance for the claim. Fly, however, was sheriff of Cochise County at the time. (ARIZONA HISTORICAL SOCIETY)

(BBB)

BILL DOOLIN GETS IT

After his dramatic escape from the Guthrie jail, Doolin hid out in the hills around Lawson, Oklahoma, where his wife and child were staying. With a $5,000 reward on his head, neighbors soon reported his nighttime comings and goings. On the night of August 24, Doolin put his wife and child in a wagon and was preparing to leave for West Texas or beyond, when he heard men west of the house and went to investigate. Hidden in a cane patch, Heck Thomas and his posse were waiting and a fuselage of buckshot and rifle fire caught the King of the Oklahoma Outlaws square in the chest. The body was taken to Guthrie and photographed for the reward money. (AC)

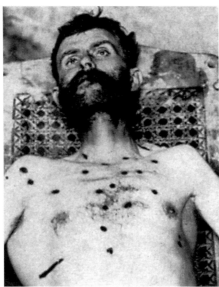

Fleming Parker
(BILL SECREST COLLECTION)

PEACH SPRINGS, ARIZONA TERRITORY
Site of the February 8, 1897 train robbery in which Fleming Parker was captured. (BEN WITTICK PHOTO, MNM)

August 13, 1896
Butch Cassidy, Elza Lay and Bob Meeks rob a bank in Montpelier, Idaho, to raise money for fellow outlaw, Matt Warner, who needs a lawyer.

August 25, 1896
At Lawson, Oklahoma, Bill Doolin is ambushed and killed by a posse led by Marshal Heck Thomas.

November 6, 1896
At Pawnee, Oklahoma, Bee Dunn is shot in the face and killed by Frank Canton, after Dunn accused Canton of spreading rumors about the way the Dunns had killed Charley Pierce and Bitter Creek Newcomb.

November 17, 1896
The Hanging Judge, Issac Parker, dies at Fort Smith, Arkansas. He was 58.

December 2, 1896
Referee Wyatt Earp is accused of throwing a prize fight in San Francisco between Bob Fitzsimmons and Tom Sharkey. [The case is thrown out of court on a technicality: prize fights are illegal in California.]

1897

The PTA (Parent-Teachers' Association) is born. Jell-O and Lifebuoy soap are introduced.

February 8, 1897
Two outlaws attempt to rob the Atlantic and Pacific Railroad at Peach Springs, Arizona. One is killed and the other, Fleming Parker, is captured.

May 9, 1897
Fleming Parker and others escape jail at Prescott, Arizona, killing an assistant county attorney in the process. Parker steals Sheriff George Ruffner's saddle horse and flees. Ruffner

catches up with Parker near Tuba City and captures him.

June 28, 1897
Kid Curry, the Sundance Kid and others rob the Butte County Bank, in Belle Forche, South Dakota.

August 23, 1897
The first Cheyenne Frontier Days celebration is held in Wyoming.

September 3, 1897
Sam Ketchum, Elza Lay and others rob a Colorado and Southern Railroad train at Folsom, New Mexico.

September 24, 1897
Kid Curry, along with the Sundance Kid and Walt Puteney are captured near Lavina, Montana.

October 31, 1897
The Sundance Kid, Harvey Logan, Walt Puteney and Tom O'Day escape jail in Deadwood, South Dakota.

December 13, 1897
At Stein's Pass, New Mexico, a Southern Pacific train is held up by the Black Jack Ketchum gang. In a furious gun battle with Wells Fargo guards, one outlaw is slain and the express is saved.

February 15, 1898
The U.S. battleship, Maine, is blown up in Havana harbor with a loss of 358 men and two officers.

April 22, 1898
The Spanish American war begins [and continues for 112 days].

June 4, 1898
Train robber, Fleming Parker, is legally hung on the courthouse plaza at Prescott. [Parker is the last person to be hung on the plaza.]

THE HANGING OF FLEMING PARKER
A crowd of invited guests watched the "Noted Cow-boy Bandit" climb the scaffold at Prescott, Arizona. The local paper reported Parker did a little jig on the trapdoor before the hood was put on and the grim sentence carried out.
(SHARLOT HALL MUSEUM)

THE INFAMOUS "SOAPY" SMITH
A former cow-boy, turned confidence man, Smith (fourth from the right) earned his nickname at Creede, Colorado, where he sold bars of soap for $5 each under the illusion some lucky buyer would find twenty dollars wrapped around his purchase. Of course, the only ones who did were shills of Smith. In 1897 Smith joined the Alaska gold rush and ran a variety of crooked scams in Skagway, where he and his gang fleeced thousands. A "Vigilance of 101" was formed to oppose him, so Soapy glibly formed the "Committee of 303," to oppose the 101. Smith was killed when he crashed a vigilance meeting on a wharf and shot it out with the city engineer. Both died. (BILL SECREST COLLECTION)

"CRIPPLE CREEK BAR-ROOM," 1898
While the Wild Bunch are robbing trains, Western themed films like "Cripple Creek Bar-Room," from the Edison studios, depict a group of actors portraying Western life. It was filmed somewhere in New Jersey. (AC)

JEFF MILTON AND GEORGE SCARBOROUGH
Two brave, effective officers of the law. Milton had a long career, retiring in 1930. Scarborough was from Louisiana and a U.S. marshal at El Paso when he killed John Selman and resigned his commission. He became a detective for the Grant County Cattlemen's Association and was shot by outlaws, possibly James Brooks (see page 101). (HALEY LIBRARY, MIDLAND, TEXAS)

July 1, 1898
In Santiago, Cuba, former lawman and mayor of Prescott, Arizona, Buckey O'Neill is killed by a sniper.

July 29, 1898
Lawmen Jeff Milton, George Scarborough and Eugene Thacker are trailing the Walters gang near Solomonville, Arizona, when they hear a shot in a nearby canyon. Riding up to investigate, the two men come face to face with "Bronco Bill" Walters, who had been firing at a rattlesnake. The outlaw fires at the officers but misses. Milton shoots Walters through the lungs. A general fight ensues with the rest of the gang and one outlaw, Kid Johnson, is wounded, dying later in the night. [Walters survives and serves a prison term.]

September 23, 1898
Jesse James, Jr. is suspected in the robbery of a Missouri Pacific train about five miles southeast of Kansas City. [James is acquitted in Feb. of 1899 and begins studying law.]

1899
The average age at death in the U.S. is 47.

May 30, 1899
Pearl Hart and her boyfriend, Joe Boot, hold up the Benson-Globe stage in Arizona and get away with $431.

June 2, 1899
The Wild Bunch robs the United Pacific's Overland Flyer at Wilcox, Wyoming.

July 11, 1899
The Ketchum gang, including William Ellsworth "Elzy" Lay, Sam Ketchum, Will Carver and Red Weaver, rob the Colorado and Southern Railroad near Folsom, New Mexico.

July 12, 1899

A posse attacks the Ketchum gang in their hideout at Turkey Creek Canyon, New Mexico. Three lawmen are killed when one of the outlaws, using smokeless powder, picks off the officers with unerring accuracy. The outlaws escape but Lay and Sam Ketchum are wounded. [Both are captured several days later and Ketchum dies from his wounds.]

August 16, 1899

Single-handedly, Tom "Black Jack" Ketchum attempts to rob the Colorado and Southern train at the, by now, familiar Folsom, N.M. site, but this time the conductor shatters Ketchum's arm with a shotgun blast and the outlaw staggers off and is found the next day, not far from the scene.

September 9, 1899

Deputy Sheriffs Burt Alvord and Billie Stiles hold up a Southern Pacific train near Cochise Station, Arizona. [They are later arrested but escape.]

November 20, 1899

Pearl Hart is tried in Florence for stage robbery. She is convicted and sentenced to five years in prison.

1900

Eastman Kodak introduces the "Brownie" box camera.
The Daisy Air Rifle (BB gun) is introduced.
Radon is discovered.

February 15, 1900

Outlaws, including "Three-Fingered Jack" Dunlap, Bravo Juan Yoas (probably Ulloa) and the Owens brothers, attempt to rob the train at Fairbank, Arizona. Unfortunately for them, the express messenger is Jeff Milton, who, after being shot in the arm, grabs a shotgun and scatters the gang with buckshot, wounding two and humiliating the rest.

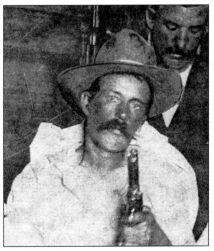

A ONE-ARMED BANDIT NAMED BLACK JACK

If Black Jack Ketchum doesn't look too happy, it's because he just had his right arm sawed off and the local wags have stuck a hat on his head and shoved an empty six-shooter in his hand, trying to coax a couple good photos out of the famous outlaw. After his attempt to rob the Folsom, N.M., train single-handedly ended in disaster (see August 16, 1899), Black Jack was taken to Trinidad, Colorado, where his right arm was amputated and these photos were taken. Note that he also got a shave and decided to keep the mustache. These photos show a different image of Black Jack than the more famous mug shot, taken at a later date (at right). It's hard to see the resemblance between the two, his latter visage being much huskier and thicker. (TOP FOUR PHOTOS BY B.D. TITSWORTH, COURTESY OF *TRUE WEST* MAGAZINE)

In his youth

Mug shot

HEADS WILL ROLL

Lawmen and officials gather around the body and severed head of Black Jack after his hanging. Various explanations have been bantied about for the macabre decapitation: the sheriff made the drop too far and Kethum's weight did the rest (from the photo the drop looks to be about par). (BILL SECREST COLLECTION)

CAUGHT IN THE ACT!

A remarkable photo of an actual stage robbery in progress! This Yosemite stage was stopped near Raymond (north of Fresno), on August 15, 1905. There were 10 passengers; six women and four men. Three of the victims (two are blacksmiths) are at right with their hands behind their backs. The robber can clearly be seen in the background, just to the left. He is wearing a battered felt hat and dirty linen duster, to hide his real clothing. When the outlaw had robbed all the passengers (yes, even the women; only the driver was spared, "I don't want a workingman's money," was his comment), a passenger named Anton Veith asked if he could take a photo. To Veith's surprise, the Bad Man answered, "Go ahead and get your camera. No one can recognize me in the get-up anyway. Hurry it up, though." The photo was published several days later in the Fresno Morning Republican.

(BILL SECREST COLLECTION)

WILD BUNCH RAIL JOB

The Tipton, Wyoming, express car destroyed by the Wild Bunch in 1900.

(UNION PACIFIC RAILROAD)

April 5, 1900

Lawman George Scarborough and a deputy are tracking an outlaw gang when the two parties collide at Triangle Springs, southwest of San Simon, Arizona. Scarborough is wounded in the leg, and while the deputy goes for help, Scarborough holds off the outlaws. [Scarborough is rescued and rushed to Deming aboard a train, but dies the following day.]

May 26, 1900

A group of outlaws identified only as "Apache County Murderers," kill two lawmen near Thompson, Utah.

June 2, 1900

A lone bandit stops three sight-seeing stagecoaches and a freight wagon in Yosemite National Park and robs the passengers. [He is never caught.]

July 7, 1900

Warren Earp is killed in a saloon by cow-boy Johnny Boyet at Wilcox, Arizona.

August 29, 1900

The Wild Bunch robs the Union Pacific near Tipton, Wyoming and gets $50.40.

September 19, 1900

Butch Cassidy and the Sundance Kid (with others) rob the First National Bank in Winnemucca, Nevada.

September 22, 1900

A lone bandit robs a passenger train in western Idaho single-handedly. Boarding at one in the morning at Sandpoint, the robber moves bunk to bunk demanding money before being chased from the train by a conductor in the day coach. [A posse trailed the outlaw to a point three miles south of Athol, but he stole a horse and vanished.]

(BBB)

November 21, 1900

The Wild Bunch sits for a formal portrait at a photography studio in Fort Worth, Texas.

The Wild Bunch, 1900 (PINKERTONS PHOTO)

1901

The first practical electric vacuum cleaner is invented in Britain.

February 1, 1901

Butch Cassidy, the Sundance Kid and Etta (her name is Ethel, Etta is a Pinkerton typo) Place rent a room at 234 West Twelfth Street in New York City.

February 20, 1901

Mr. and Mrs. Harry Place (Sundance and Ethel) and James T. Ryan (Butch Cassidy) sail for Buenos Aires, Argentina, on the S.S. Herminius.

March 25, 1901

The Arizona Rangers are established at Phoenix, Arizona.

April 26, 1901

Black Jack Ketchum is legally hung at Clayton, New Mexico.

June 12, 1901

Suspected of horse theft, Gregorio Cortez shoots and kills Sheriff "Brack" Morris 10 miles south of Kennedy, Texas. [After a massive manhunt, Cortez is finally captured on June 22. See sidebar.]

June 17, 1901

Stage robber Bill Miner is released into the Twentieth Century after serving 20 years in San Quentin.

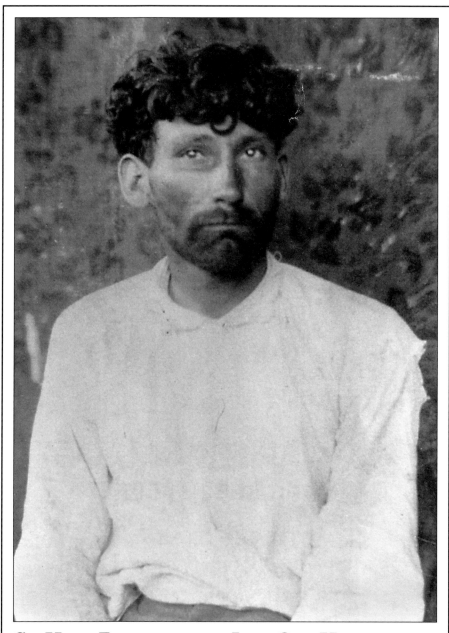

So Many Rangers, for Just One Mexican

After the massive manhunt to bring him in (see June 12, 1901), Gregorio Cortez was first tried and found innocent of the murder of Sheriff Morris. His defense was the confusion of the Spanish translation: When told by the translator he and his brother were being arrested, Gregorio responded in Spanish, "You cannot arrest me for nothing." This was translated to the sheriff as, "No one can arrest me." Based on this comment, the sheriff drew his gun and the tragic events unfolded. After numerous court battles (Cortez spent time in 11 different county jails), he was sentenced to 99 years. Cortez served 12 years before being pardoned in 1913. Along the way, Gregorio had become a folk hero on both sides of the border. "The Ballad of Gregorio Cortez" sang the praises of "the seventh son of a seventh son" who had something akin to mystical powers. "Then said Gregorio Cortez, with his pistol in his hand," went one of the verses, "Ah, so many Rangers just to take one Mexican." After his release, Cortez went to Mexico where he was received as a hero. (PHOTO COURTESY OF AL RITTER)

THE ARIZONA RANGERS, 1901
The legendary "26 Men" rode the backtrails of Arizona Territory and did much to clean out pockets of lawlessness. Captain Thomas Rynning is third from left. (MCLAUGHLIN COLLECTION)

A FREE MAN
Cole Younger's mug shot on the day he was released from prison. (AC)

TOM HORN BRAIDS HIS TIME
Prisoner Tom Horn poses with one of the fine horsehair braids he wove while waiting in jail.
(BOB MCCUBBIN COLLECTION)

THE BEGINNING OF THE DECLINE
Authorities reported only 22 train robberies for the year 1902. Outlaws everywhere were being rounded up, shot down and put out of business. In Arizona a curious outlaw made the news: According to lawman Heck Thomas, outlaw Tom King was killed in a holdup in a border town near Tombstone. Upon burial he turned out to be a woman. It was actually Flora Quick, alias, Flora Mundis, Chinese Dot. Evidently, she had an unhappy marriage and fled westward, donned men's attire and started her own gang around Clifton, Arizona. On Tom King's reward circular it read: figure is "faultless" but he is "badly tanned." (BBB)

July 3, 1901
The Wild Bunch, sans Butch & Sundance, rob the Great Northern Railroad at Wagner, Montana.

July 11, 1901
Cole and James Younger are paroled from prison in Stillwater, Minnesota, after serving 25 years.

September 6, 1901
President William McKinley is shot at point-blank range during a visit to the Pan-American Exposition at Buffalo, New York.

October 29, 1901
A train carrying Buffalo Bill's Wild West Show wrecks near Lexington, North Carolina. Among the injured is Annie Oakely [who spends several months in the hospital].

December 15, 1901
Harvey Logan is arrested near Knoxville, Tennessee.

April 2, 1902
Thomas Tally opens the first moving-picture theatre at 262 South Main St., in Los Angeles.

April 15, 1902
Wild Bunch member, O.C. "Deaf Charley" Hanks is slain while resisting arrest by three policemen in a San Antonio saloon brawl.

May 13, 1902
Allegedly the first pornographic movies in the West are shown in Denver by the Colorado Mutoscope Company.

June 9, 1902
Outlaw Harry Tracy kills three guards and escapes from the Oregon State prison.

August 5, 1902
In a huge manhunt, Harry Tracy kills four more men before he is trapped by a posse near Davenport, Washington and shot dead.

October 26, 1902

Tom Horn is found guilty of killing 14-year-old Willie Nickell at Cheyenne, Wyoming.

November 18, 1902

The *Washington Evening Star* runs an illustration of President "Teddy" Roosevelt refusing to shoot a mother bear while hunting in Mississippi. With the president's permission, a couple who operate a candy store in Brooklyn, N.Y. begin manufacturing a brown plush toy they call The Teddy Bear.

November 21, 1902

At Solomonville, Arizona, bandit Augustin Chacon is hanged for murder and numerous stage robberies.

1903

The first Harley Davidson rolls off the line.
The first automobile to complete a cross-country trip arrives in New York from San Francisco.
The historic journey takes 63 days.

January 16, 1903

President Teddy Roosevelt commutes Henry Starr's 15-year sentence and he is released on the promise to be good. [Starr travels to Tulsa to help his mother run a cafe.]

April 19, 1903

Desperado and killer Jim McKinney is trapped in a Chinese joss house in Bakersfield, California. McKinney kills two lawmen before he is slain.

June 27, 1903

Harvey Logan pulls off a daring escape from jail in Knoxville, Tennessee, making headlines coast to coast.

July, 1903

The bank in Cody, Wyoming, is robbed and blamed on Logan and the Wild Bunch.

"THE GREAT TRAIN ROBBERY," 1903
Although often credited as the first Western (several films including Cripple Creek Barroom *and* Kit Carson *preceeded it), The Great Train Robbery was an instant smash with audiences everywhere. When actor George Barnes (above) silently aimed his revolver out of the screen, "women put their fingers in their ears to shut out the noise of the gunfire." Grown men ducked and females screamed. The Bad Man on the Big Screen, had arrived.* (AC)

TAP DUNCAN, ON THE DIAMOND BAR, 1903
Arizona cattleman, movie promoter, legend and owner of the Diamond Bar ranch in northern Mohave County, Tap Duncan was a friend to the Wild Bunch. When Harvey Logan was killed near Rifle, Colorado, he was using the alias, "Tap Duncan." And when Black Jack Ketchum was hung, the newspapers reported a persistent rumor of a gang of cow-boys led by "Tap Duncan" were going to liberate the Bad Man and set him free. (AC)

SURROUNDED BY A NEW WORLD
Tom Horn and another prisoner made a brief escape on August 10, 1903, but Horn was quickly recaptured. Unfortunately his attempt convinced many (notably the judicial community) he was guilty. (AMERICAN HERITAGE CENTER, UNIVERSITY OF WYOMING)

Arkansas Tom

ARKANSAS TOM DAUGHERTY

Raised in Missouri, in a religous family (two of his brothers became preachers), Roy Daugherty went the other way, running away from home at 14, calling himself "Tom Jones" he told everyone he was from Arkansas. He hired on at an Oklahoma ranch and it was there he received the nickname "Arkansas Tom." Cow-boying didn't pay enough, so in the 1890s he joined Bill Doolin's gang of bank robbers. He was captured after the infamous gunfight at Ingall's, convicted and sentenced to a 50-year prison term. Through the efforts of his preacher brothers he was paroled in 1910. For two years he ran a restaurant in Drumright, Oklahoma. He was a participant in the filming of "The Passing of the Oklahoma Outlaw," produced by lawmen E.D. Nix, Bill Tilghman and Chris Madsen, playing himself. Much to his family's chagrin, the aging bank robber was involved in a bank robbery at Neosho, Missouri and served another term in prison. Released once more, he was in on another bank job at Asbury, Missouri. The end came when Tom took on a different kind of job. (GLENN SHIRLEY)

August 9, 1903
Tom Horn and another prisoner attempt to escape from jail in Cheyenne, Wyoming. Horn is slightly wounded and both are captured and returned to jail.

September 23, 1903
Bill Miner and his gang rob an express train near Portland, Oregon.

November 20, 1903
Tom Horn is hung.

December, 1903
Authorities report only 13 train robberies for the year.

1904
Japan decisively defeats Russia in a naval war using a new class of weapons: self-propelled torpedoes, land mines, and machine guns.

June 7, 1904
Harvey Logan and two others rob the Denver & Rio Grande train near Parachute, Colorado (they get very little).

June 8, 1904
Near Rifle, Colorado, a posse closes in on a wounded outlaw and he commits suicide. He is identified as "Tap Duncan" and buried. Later, he is dug up and identified as Harvey Logan, alias Kid Curry.

Harvey Logan
(PINKERTONS PHOTO)

August 14, 1904
Tucson, Arizona, police begin a series of raids designed to close the city's opium dens. [Several months later the city council increases gambling license fees to exorbitant levels, in an attempt to drive out all gambling houses.]

September 10, 1904

"Old Bill" Miner and two others pull off Canada's first train robbery at Mission Junction, British Columbia.

November 21, 1904

Motor-driven omnibuses replace horse-drawn carriages in Paris, France.

1905

Zane Grey publishes his first Western, The Spirit of the Border.

January 9, 1905

On orders from the czar, Russian demonstrators are machine-gunned in front of the Winter Palace at St. Petersburg. It will become known as "Bloody Sunday."

January 15, 1905

The Arizona Rangers report to the governor they have made 1,058 arrests in 24 months.

February 14, 1905

In Argentina, two unidentified "Yankees" hold up the Banco de Tarapacá Y Argentino in Rio Gallegos and get off with 20,000 pesos. Butch and Sundance are suspected and chased out of the country.

March 15, 1905

Two train robbers, Vernon and George Gates, are shot to death when officers attempt to arrest them in a hotel room at Lordsburg, New Mexico.

October 4, 1905

President Calvin Coolidge marries Grace A. Goodhue.

December 19, 1905

Butch Cassidy, the Sundance Kid, Ethel Place and an unidentified accomplice hold up the Banco de la Nacion in Villa Mercede, Argentina, escaping with 12,000 pesos.

MAP OF SOUTH AMERICA AND BUTCH CASSIDY ROBBERIES
Butch read about favoriable Argentine ranching conditions in *National Geographic* magazine. For some time the outlaw trio, Butch, Sundance and Ethel (Etta) lived peacefully at Cholila. Butch wrote home he had 300 head of cattle, 1,500 sheep and 28 good saddle horses. Unfortunately, the good life didn't last and the Boy's luck ran out at San Vincente, Bolivia. The site of their Villa Mercedes bank robbery is also shown.
(HAND DRAWN MAP, BOB STEINHILBER)

THE TEA PARTY PHOTO
This amazing photo shows the Sundance Kid, Ethel (Etta) Place and Butch Cassidy getting ready to have tea on their Cholila ranch in 1903. The photo was sent to a family member and remained in the family for many years until it was published in 1992. (COPYRIGHTED PAUL D. ERNST PHOTO)

"THE LIFE OF A COW-BOY," 1906

As scores of Western themed movies tried to cash in on the success of The Great Train Robbery, *holdups of every kind began to see their way onto the screen. This still from* The Life of a Cow-boy, *1906, depicts a stagecoach robbery in progress. Other scenes from the movie included a saloon interior and a chase on horseback.* (AC)

ARIZONA RANGER, HARRY WHEELER

A Texas cow-boy who was recruited for the newly formed Arizona Rangers, Wheeler was quite effective along the Arizona-Mexico border and was later sheriff of Cochise County. (AC)

HENRY STARR

On his first holdup "job" Henry Starr's horse ran into a barbed wire fence in the dark and the authorities traced the saddle back to him. He would slip through the justice system many times in his career. (GLENN SHIRLEY)

December, 1905
Authorities report only seven train robberies for the year.

1906
The Mack truck, the Victrola and the electric washing machine are introduced.

April 18, 1906
An earthquake strikes San Francisco, killing more than 3,000 people and destroying more than 28,000 buildings. Casualty figures are altered and underreported by local officials, who are afraid Eastern bankers will panic and ruin San Francisco's credit rating.

1907
Marion Morrison (John Wayne) is born.

February 28, 1907
Arizona Ranger Harry Wheeler prevents a double murder, and, although twice wounded, kills the assailant on the main street of Benson, Arizona.

February 29, 1908
Pat Garrett is murdered near Las Cruces, New Mexico by a 31-year-old cow-boy named Wayne Brazel.

March 13, 1908
Henry Starr and Kid Wilson rob the State Bank in Tyro, Kansas, of $2,500. [There have been rumors that Starr has been holding up banks previously in Missouri and Oklahoma. In June, Starr and Wilson cross over into Colorado and rob another bank, then split up.]

November 6, 1908
Butch Cassidy and the Sundance Kid are killed in a shootout in San Vicente, Bolivia.

(BBB)

April 1, 1909

Tucson, Arizona, police warn motorists to observe the municipal speed limit of seven miles per hour.

April 19, 1909

Jim "Killer" Miller and the three ranchers who hired him are lynched in Ada, Oklahoma.

May 11, 1909

Henry Starr is arrested in Bosque (a small mining camp 17 miles southwest of Phoenix), Arizona and returned to Lamar, Colorado.

June 28, 1909

A masked man holds up the crew of a streetcar at the gates of the University of Arizona, in Tucson.

October 7, 1909

One of the last horseback manhunts in the West ends on California's Mojave Desert when fugitive, Paiute Indian Willie Boy, commits suicide.

December 25, 1909

Mexican Rurales fight a desperate gun battle with six horse thieves who have been the scourge of the Arizona border. Four outlaws are killed and two wounded.

1910

Bonnie Parker [as in Bonnie & Clyde] is born in Rowena, Texas.

May 12, 1910

Two boy bandits on horseback, rob a Maricopa and Phoenix train near Gila crossing, but are quickly rounded up by a sheriff who chases them down in an automobile.

November 25, 1910

Henry Starr pleads guilty and is sentenced from seven to 25 years at Canon City penitentiary.

ARIZONA RANGERS & RURALES, 1905
Colonel Kosterlitzky (on white horse) and his Sonoran Rurales straddle the border with the Arizona Rangers, led by Thomas Rynning (third from left with white gauntlets). The two groups aided each other often in the capture of Bad Men along the international line. (MCLAUGHLIN COLLECTION)

"A lie can be half-way round the world before the truth can get its boots on."
—JAMES CALLAGHAN

THE TALL TEXAN LAUNCHED INTO ETERNITY
The Lady's Man of the Wild Bunch, Ben Kilpatrick (left and at left in photo below), went out in embarrassing *style.* (LEFT PHOTO, PINKERTONS PHOTO; PHOTO BELOW, SOUTHERN PACIFIC RAILROAD)

PANCHO VILLA

Born to peasant stock in the northern Mexican state of Durango, Villa became a bandit at an early age, then graduated to revolutionary. In the revolt of 1910-11, he was largely responsible for the triumph of Fancisco Madero over President Porfirio Diaz. (AC) Along the way Villa amassed a small fortune from his "military" excursions. Villa shocked the United States when he raided Columbus, New Mexico, on March 9, 1916, killing 17 Americans. The reasons for the raid are obscure and disputed. One week later, the U.S. sent John "Blackjack" Pershing into Mexico with 10,000 men, pursuing Villa all across Chihuahua for a year without success. Pancho eventually "retired" to Chihuahua City to an impressive estate, but the rumors of his return haunted Mexican politics for years. (TOP PHOTO, NATIONAL ARCHIVES)

A VILLISTA
One of Pancho's fighters. (AC)

February 22, 1911
Bill Miner and two other outlaws rob a train at White Suphur, Georgia. A posse captures the gang and Miner is sent back to prison.

September 11, 1911
Free liquor passed out at Republican headquarters in Tucson, Arizona, results in two shootings.

October 4, 1911
Four masked men rob the wrong train four miles out of Okesa, Oklahoma. Instead of several thousand dollars (which was on the *next* train), the thieves, led by Elmer McCurdy, get $46 and two bottles of whiskey.

October 7, 1911
A very drunk Elmer McCurdy is surrounded by lawmen in a barn on the Big Caney. "It took an hour before he dropped," a deputy told the newspaper, meaning from bullets, not whiskey. [The outlaw's body was taken to Pawhuska, embalmed and displayed to the public, pending arrival of relatives. Thus began the strange journey of Elmer McCurdy's body!]

January 12, 1912
A running gun battle in Phoenix, Arizona, ends in the capture of a gang of outlaws who had been terrifying the town for weeks. [Three days later, the first annual Phoenix Auto Show is held.]

March 13, 1912
The last active member of the Wild Bunch, Ben Kilpatrick, tries to rob a Southern Pacific train near Sanderson, Texas. When the veteran train robber turns his head, the messenger hits him on the back of the head with an ice mallet, killing him. Ben's partner, Ole Beck, appears and is killed with one shot.

April 14, 1912

The world's largest passenger liner, the Titanic, strikes an iceberg in the north Atlantic and sinks. 706 people, mostly women and children survive. 1,517 perish.

September 2, 1913

After two prison breaks and a body weakened by illness, 67-year-old outlaw, Bill Miner, dies in the state prison at Milledgeville, Georgia.

Bill Miner

(PINKERTONS PHOTO)

September 24, 1913

Henry Starr is paroled on the stipulation that he report once a month and not leave Colorado (see sidebar).

September 8, 1914

Henry Starr robs the Keystone State Bank of $3,000.

September 30, 1914

Henry Starr robs the Kiefer Central Bank in Keifer, Oklahoma, of $6,400.

October 6, 1914

Henry Starr robs the Farmers' National Bank at Tupelo, Oklahoma, of $800.

October 14, 1914

Henry Starr robs the Pontotoc Bank at Pontotoc, Oklahoma, of $1,100.

October 20, 1914

Henry Starr robs the Byars State Bank at Byars, Oklahoma, of $700.

November 13, 1914

Henry Starr robs the Farmers' State Bank at Glencoe, Oklahoma, of $2,400.

November 20, 1914

Henry Starr robs the Citizens' State Bank at Wardville, Oklahoma, of $800.

"I must have excitement."
—HENRY STARR

Photo by J.L. Rivkin © Tulsa 1914

"THE BAD MAN FROM OKLAHOMA" GOES BAD, AGAIN

Henry Starr was a model prisoner at the Canon City Penitentiary. He worked on the roads, was a trustee in charge of a work gang, and was given a weapon and a horse and his duties sometimes took him 200 miles from the prison without supervision. He studied law in the prison library (officials claimed he could have passed the state bar easily). He wrote his autobiography: *Thrilling Events, Life of Henry Starr,* and, overall, seemed the perfect candidate for a normal life back to society.

Paroled in September of 1913, Starr opened a small short-order cafe at Holly, Colorado, but it didn't last. People were afraid of him and called him "the bad man from Oklahoma." A pretty, brunette who was married to a local merchant became enchanted with the former outlaw. When their affair became public, Starr closed his cafe and the two fled the state. Detectives and law enforcement officials reported sightings of the two in Arizona and Nevada.

Somewhere in the next several months, Starr teamed up with a partner and began a bank robbing tear that would shock the nation. (GLENN SHIRLEY COLLECTION)

ONE SWANKY HIDEOUT

While posses scoured the rural areas of Oklahoma, hoping to flush out the notorious bank robber, Henry Starr was holed up with his Honey in the heart of Tulsa, at 1534 East Second Street, in a modern five-room bungalow with electric lights, hot and cold running water, bath and telephone. In the garage was a five-passenger Dodge, which Starr reportedly liked to go on nightly "joy rides" around town. He especially enjoyed going to the moving picture houses. The final insult: the Tulsa county sheriff lived two blocks away.

PAUL CURRY
The boy who shot Henry Starr with a hog gun (he is holding Starr's rifle).
(GLENN SHIRLEY COLLECTION)

OKLAHOMA OUTLAW SLANG

"Barkers"—pistols, as in, "After the robbery we were in the saddle and set our barkers to snarling to keep the locals at bay."

"Tick Birds"—hangers on, who lived off the table scraps of the outlaws.

"Armed to the Teeth?"—On his third "job" Henry Starr claimed he and another outlaw were armed with only "an old white-handled .45 and three cartridges" between them.

December 16, 1914
Henry Starr robs the Prue State Bank at Prue, Oklahoma, of $1,400.

December 29, 1914
Henry Starr robs the Carney State Bank at Carney, Oklahoma, of $2,853. [The newspaper reports Starr and his accomplice "marched their victims to the edge of town, entered a buggy (hitched in a grove of trees) and struck off across the country."]

January 4, 1915
Henry Starr robs the Oklahoma State Bank at Preston, of $1,200.

January 5, 1915
Henry Starr robs the First National Bank at Owasso, Oklahoma, of $1,500.

January 12, 1915
Henry Starr robs two banks: the First National Bank at Terlton, Oklahoma, of $1,800; then he hits the Garber State Bank in Garber, Oklahoma, and gets $2,500.

January 13, 1915
Henry Starr robs the Vera State bank of $1,300. [From here, Henry and Laura go to Tulsa to reside. See sidebar.]

February 8, 1915
D.W. Griffith's motion picture "Birth of A Nation" premiers in Los Angeles.

February 18, 1915
Frank James dies at his home in Missouri.

March 27, 1915
Henry Starr and six others rob the Stroud State Bank and the First National Bank simultaneously. Starr is hit in the left thigh with a shot fired by 17-year-old Paul Curry. Another robber is hit in the neck by Curry. Both are captured.

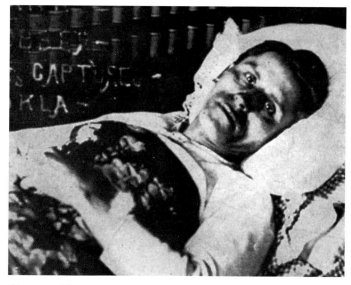

STARR RECOVERING
As soon as Starr was captured, Bill Tilghman and his film crew raced to Stroud to get moving pictures of the outlaw. This is a still from the film. (GLENN SHIRLEY COLLECTION)

April 23, 1915

German troops introduce a new weapon on the battlefields of Europe: poison gas.

August 2, 1915

Henry Starr pleads guilty and is sentenced to 25 years in the Oklahoma State Penitentiary.

November 11, 1918

World War I ends with a horrific scorecard. Killed in the conflict: 1.8 million Germans, 1.7 million Russians, 1.4 million French, 1.2 million Austrians and Hungarians, 850,000 British, 460,000 Italians, 325,000 Turks, and 115,000 Americans. In addition to the deaths, some 20 million have been blinded, maimed, mutilated, crippled, permanently shell-shocked or disabled.

1919

Dial telephones are introduced.

March 15, 1919

Henry Starr is pardoned and goes into the movie business.

TEDDY ROOSEVELT (AC)

February 24, 1919

Thanks to the efforts of Teddy Roosevelt, all 1.2 million acres of the Grand Canyon National Park is established.

PAN-AMERICAN MOTION PICTURE CORP. PRESENTS

Henry Starr

---IN---

A DEBTOR TO THE LAW

A MOVIE STILL AND POSTER FROM STARR'S "A DEBTOR TO THE LAW." (POSTER, AC; MOVIE STILL, BOB McCUBBIN COLLECTION)

WHAT DID IT FEEL LIKE TO ROB A BANK?

Henry Starr claimed outlaws constantly feared treachery. It was what turned the James and Youngers away from the bank at Mankato. Starr remembered when he stepped into the train station at Nowata, Oklahoma, for his first job and saw a half dozen men in the office, "in an instant fear that there had been treachery was gnawing at my heart. It is a fear that constantly faces all who play the game."

HENRY STARR, THE STAR
A publicity still for, "A Debtor to the Law" with Starr in full Bad Man gear. (BOB MCCUBBIN COLLECTION)

1920

Bills are introduced into Congress to prohibit the shipment of motion picture films "purporting to show the acts of ex-convicts, desperadoes, bandits, train robbers, bank robbers or outlaws."

February 18, 1921

Henry Starr and three others rob the People's National Bank at Harrison, Arkansas and get away with $6,000, but Starr is shot [and dies three days later].

1924

One of the last of the holdup men, Arkansas Tom, is shot while babysitting. (See below.)

TILGHMAN & ARKANSAS TOM

The noted outlaw, Arkansas Tom, actually went on tour with Tilghman but he told the aging lawman, the road made him feel "restless." Tilghman got the former outlaw a job with Chris Madsen in Kansas City, but he soon fell into his old habits. (GLENN SHIRLEY COLLECTION)

AL JENNINGS IN WORKING GEAR

The Oklahoma Bad Man made several movies about his life. (CURTIS PUBLISHING CO.)

REEL BAD MEN VS. THE REAL DEAL

"[Movie] Producers have the idea that a gang of 'bad men' have to be fantastically masked, carry a whole arsenal in plain sight, plan for days on the details of the robbery, and carry it out with several hundred feet of thrills and romance.

"Let me tell you how it was actually done in those days. We didn't wear masks and we didn't carry our guns where they could be seen. There was very little bloodshed and no killing except in running fights. When my brother Frank and I decided to relieve a bank of some of its bullion, we went in quietly, he covered the cashier while I took the bags from the safe, then we'd lock up the cashiers in the vault for safe keeping.

"There wasn't any glamour in the life; there was much that was bad, much that was indifferent, and some that was good. But there wasn't any romance about it. It was hard, sordid and tragic."

—Al Jennings, in above photo (MUSEUM OF MODERN ART)

ROAD SHOW

Lawman Bill Tilghman hit the road with his "Passing of the Oklahoma Outlaws" film. He would rent a hall, lecture, show the movie, pack up and drive to another town and do it all over again. He's seen here (at right with vest) in Detroit, hawking his wares.

SHOOT 'EM UP

Although Tilghman (above) had the right idea with his movies, the production qualities of the surviving footage is quite weak. There are no closeups or jump cuts and most of the action is filmed from a distance. His posters (below) were decent and seem to have been done by professionals. Unfortunately no copy of "Passing of the Oklahoma Outlaws" has been found. (ABOVE TWO PHOTOS AND TWO POSTERS BELOW, WESTERN HISTORY COLLECTIONS, UNIVERSITY OF OKLAHOMA LIBRARY)

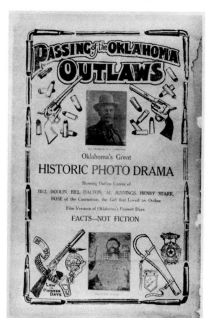

TILGHMAN'S MOVIE POSTERS

"The Bank Robbery," 1908

Cache, Oklahoma, was all abuzz in August of 1908 as the Oklahoma Mutoscope Company began filming a mock robbery at the local bank. The film company allegedly was organized with capital stock of $50,000 and W.E. Curtis of Kansas City had "the most perfect picture machine in the world." But, as is the case even today, money and a good camera doesn't make a good movie. However, numerous legendary lawmen and outlaws show up in the picture: Chief Quanah Parker, Al Jennings, Bill Tilghman, Heck Thomas, Chris Madsen and possibly Frank Canton can be seen in the movie. Here are several stills from the film: (JEFF MOREY COLLECTION)

Al Jennings and Bill Tilghman

Frank Canton, (?) and Heck Thomas

Chris Madsen   **Quanah Parker**

(AC)

BRONCHO BILLY MAKES GOOD

The first star of Westerns was an unlikely character named Max Aronson. After changing his name to Anderson in hopes of getting into vaudeville, he appeared in *The Great Train Robbery,* in 1903 (he may have appeared in as many as four different roles), and became convinced his future was in the movies.

Travelling to California, Anderson realized the westerns being made didn't have a central character, so he scouted around Niles (about 400 miles north of Los Angeles), looking for someone with equestrian talents. Finding nobody to his liking, he settled on himself (an odd choice considering he was a terrible rider). As Broncho Billy, Anderson began churning out a new film each week. He was writer, director and star of more than 375 such films made between 1908 and 1915.

WILLIAM S. HART

Born in 1870, Hart became a stage actor at age 17 and did 20 years of Shakespeare and classical roles before he came west and started his "cow-boy" career. He was also a competition walker, a popular sport around the first of the century. Hart began his motion picture career in 1915, and developed the "Good-Bad Man" character that helped define later movie roles from Billy the Kid to Mannix. From 1915 to 1925 he was the most popular Western star, but with the arrival of flashier cow-boys like Tom Mix (see next page), Hart's star began a decline. He finally signed off with his final major picture "Tumbleweeds" and rode off into the sunset. Although retired he wrote several young people's books and an autobiography and died at Newall, California, on his small ranch, now a park. (AC)

Low Slung Guns

The budget for each film was about $800 and each one grossed nearly $50,000! Anderson became the first star and the first actor to be given screen credit and the first actor to use a stuntman to take his falls.

The Broncho Billy films were the first Western serials, and many of the titles appear to have been pulled out of a hat: *Broncho Billy and the Baby, Broncho Billy's Love Affair, Broncho Billy and the Greaser, Broncho Billy's Oath, Broncho Billy's Mexican Wife, Broncho Billy's Leap, Broncho Billy's Christian Spirit, Broncho Billy's Bible, Broncho Billy's Last Spree* and *Broncho Billy's Christmas Dinner.*

Unfortunately, Anderson tired of life on the range, tried to do comedy and failed. He died broke and alone in 1971.

ALL OVER THE ROAD
Broncho Billy (above center), *parlayed the first portrayal of the "good Bad Man" into a fat paycheck. Although his film character lacked any consistency—sometimes he was a doctor, sometimes an alcoholic, sometimes he was religious, sometimes he even died at the end—but no matter what happened, Broncho Billy was back the next week, bigger and better.*
(AC)

TOM MIX
Born in Pennsylvania, Mix got his start with the Miller Brothers' 101 Ranch out of Oklahoma, trick riding and performing in their shows. Mix made the transition to movies around 1909 and was known for his flashy clothes and stunts. He signaled the arrival of the showman Bad Man. He reportedly was making $15,000 a week in 1915 (with no taxes!). He and his faithful horse Tony (a star of his own movie) were the predicessor of many stars to come. He was killed in 1940, near Florence, Arizona, in an auto accident. (AC)

"In many foreign countries, the Western movie, with its portrayal of valor, indomitablility, and often summary justice, is the very image of America, the mirror in which they see the reflection of our greatest virtues and worst excesses."
—TED SENNETT,
GREAT HOLLYWOOD WESTERNS, 1990

COLONEL TIM MCCOY

A Wyoming cow-boy from Michigan, McCoy was a cavalry officer in World War I rising to the rank of lieutenant colonel. In 1922, McCoy served as the techical director for the film, *The Covered Wagon*. After the release of the movie, he was sent out on the road to promote the film and he did so well, Metro-Goldwyn-Mayer hired him to do a series of Westerns. McCoy was a top star for a decade, tried a Western circus (which failed), then served in World War II in the Air Force, rising to the rank of colonel and earning a bronze star and other commendations. After the war, McCoy returned to making Western movies and did considerable television work. When asked what his favorite film had been he replied, "I don't know. They paid me to make 'em, not watch 'em." McCoy was the first movie cow-boy to dress all in black and he was no doubt the inspiration for Hopalong Cassidy's outift. Colonel Tim retired to a ranchito near Nogales, Arizona and died at the Fort Huachuca military hospital in 1978.

(BOTH PHOTOS, AC)

JESSE JAMES AT THE MOVIES

(AC)

Jesse James is the only Bad Man to be portrayed on film by his real son. In 1921, Jesse James, Jr. (whose real name was Jesse Edwards James, he was not a true Junior), starred in the two first motion pictures about his late father; *Jesse James Under the Black Flag* and *Jesse James As the Outlaw*. 18 years later, one of Jesse Junior's four daughters, Jo Frances, helped write the screenplay for the Twentieth Century Fox movie, *Jesse James*, starring Tyrone Power and Henry Fonda.

There have been over thirty films made about Jesse James. In fact, he is second only to Billy the Kid in celluloid adulation (the Kid has 48 and counting).

A wide range of actors have portrayed Jesse on the wide screen, including Tyrone Power, Roy Rogers, Rod Cameron, Clayton Moore (of Lone Ranger fame), Dale Robertson, Audie Murphy, Robert Wagner, Robert Duval and Rob Lowe.

Likewise, Frank James has been played by more than a few notables, including the aforementoned Henry Fonda and Bill Paxton.

BREAKING OUT OF THE WEST

Very few people knew who they were before the release of the movie "Butch Cassidy and the Sundance Kid" in 1969. Both outlaws had faded from the landscape and only a few regional history buffs carried their banner. But the acclaimed film, written by William Goldman, and starring Paul Newman and Robert Redford, launched the two train robbers straight out of obscurity and directly into the pantheon of legendary Western Bad Men.

The film is extraordinary on several accounts: for one, the New York sojourn is related in a series of 300 still photos with no dialogue, only silent movie type music on the soundtrack. And it works! Also, no one had ever left the West in a movie before. The studio (20th Century-Fox) was befuddled by this: Roy Rogers never left the West. John Wayne never left the West. Will audiences accept them going to Bolivia?

Accept it they did, as the movie has become one of the favorite Westerns of all time, and, as the disclaimer at the beginning proclaims, "Not that it matters, but most of what follows is true." And, incredibly for Hollywood, it mostly is.

"Damn-it-all, why is everything we're good at illegal?"
—BUTCH CASSIDY,
PLAYED BY PAUL NEWMAN IN *BUTCH CASSIDY AND THE SUNDANCE KID*

SECOND TO NONE, FOURTH IN LINE
The classic movie poster which shows Butch and Sundance forever frozen in time. Ironicaly, Redford was not the first choice to play Sundance. Marlon Brando was too busy with social causes to act. Next, the studio tried to get Warren Beatty and then Steve McQueen. Fourth in line came Redford, who made the signature role the namesake of his Sundance Film Festival. (AC)

You never met a pair like Butch and The Kid

They're Taking Trains...
They're Taking Banks
And They're Taking
One Piece Of Baggage!

20th Century-Fox presents
PAUL NEWMAN
ROBERT REDFORD
KATHARINE ROSS

BUTCH CASSIDY AND THE SUNDANCE KID

A George Roy Hill–Paul Monash Production. Co-Starring STROTHER MARTIN, JEFF COREY, HENRY JONES.
Executive Producer PAUL MONASH Produced by JOHN FOREMAN Directed by GEORGE ROY HILL Written by WILLIAM GOLDMAN
Music Composed and Conducted by BURT BACHARACH A NEWMAN-FOREMAN Presentation PANAVISION® COLOUR BY DE LUXE

THE WEST ITSELF BECOMES A STAR:

Thanks to the East

If you have been following along, you realize much of the crime in the Old West was way too similiar to crime in the modern world—East or West!

The point being, my wife is right (Ouch!): If you take almost any crime of the 1880s and put it out on the Plains, or in the Rocky Mountains, or on the flaming deserts of the Southwest, add a "fleet horse" and a "trusty six-shooter," both of which "run together like molasses," you've got romance where mere criminality once stood.

And, ironically, many of the romantic legends of the Old West Bad Men emanated from the East. Each time another family moved from the farm to the city, the blossoming pulp industry seemed to gain more avid customers. These newcomers, who were streaming to the hard streets of the eastern metropolises, desired to read about people like themselves, rural heroes who defied convention.

So the outlaw's freedom in a land lavished with plenty of room to roam became especially compelling. In fact, the more crowded it got in the tenement slums of the eastern cities, the more they seemed to enjoy reading Wild West adventure.

Since then, the legends and myths about Bad Men have accumulated like tailings from a strip mine (and to some revisionist historians, about as appealing).

Still, as author Jay Hyams explains, "As hard as it is today to look back and believe, some of their stories are true."

The trick, of course, is determining which ones.

"It takes two Easterners to believe one Westerner."
—OLD VAQUERO SAYING

Many Bad Men were fruitcakes. **True**

Gunfighters wore tie down holsters like this. **Not true**

Bad Men wore rolled up levis like this. **Not true**

Billy the Kid: killed 21 men, one for each year of his life. **Not true**

(AC)

TALL (TALES) IN THE SADDLE

Ambushed by the Rogers gang and galloping at unheard-of speeds, Mustang Sam stood up on his mount's back and taking aim, eliminated each of his pursuers one by one. **Not True:** *based on a dime novel character this illustration appeared on a collector series of Coors Beer cans in 1998 (at right).* (BBB)

THE OK MORAL

Generation after generation tells the same story over and over again. Why keep retelling it? To reach the end of a collective mourning? That the retelling might undo the past and make it happen differently?

One story that keeps getting retold is the so-called Gunfight at the O.K. Corral, which seems to be gaining in numbers of retellings rather than reaching the end. No less than two dozen movies and TV shows have dealt with the controversial 30 seconds in Tombstone, including *Star Trek*, episode 56, *Spector of the Gun*.

Two recent movies, *Tombstone*, 1993 and *Wyatt Earp*, 1994 did much to revive the Western movie and expose a whole new generation to the Bad Man genre.

Wyatt Earp as a movie character is third on the list of most portrayed gunfighters (27), after Jesse James and Billy the Kid.

Stars who have played the legendary Earp include Errol Flynn, Randolph Scott, Walter Huston, Henry Fonda, Ronald Reagan, Rory Calhoun, Joel McCrea, Burt Lancaster, Hugh O'Brian, James Stewart, James Garner, Bruce Willis (playing Tom Mix portraying Wyatt Earp), Kevin Costner and Kurt Russell (in photo below). (TOUCHSTONE PICTURES)

HENRY MCCARTY STANDS TALL

When it comes to movies, one Bad Man reigns supreme: Billy the Kid. More Westerns have been made about this little waif than any other character (48 and counting!).

Johnny Mack Brown (above) starred as the Kid in the 1930 version, *Billy the Kid*. Other stars who have taken a shot at little Billy include Joel McCrae, Bob Steele, Roy Rogers, Robert Taylor, Buster Crabbe, Lash LaRue, Audie Murphy, Paul Newman, Marlon Brando, Kris Kristofferson, Michael J. Pollard, Emilio Estevev, Joel Grey, Dennis Hopper, Robert Vaughn and Val Kilmer. (AC)

December 7, 1976

In a fun house on The Pike at Long Beach, California, a television crew filming an episode of "Six Million Dollar Man" makes a grisly discovery. When a grip goes to move what he thinks is an artificial mummy, an arm breaks off, and to his horror, he notices, what appears to be, a human bone sticking out.

The fire inspector is called and he declares it is a human being, albeit, one covered with gobs of shellac, wax and a pinkish paint that glows in the dark.

An autopsy is ordered, which reveals a bullet hole and a "half-jacket, copperjacket bullet in the left entail." Doctors also find ticket stubs, in his mouth. One of them reads: Louis Sonney's Museum of Crime: 521 S. Main St., Los Angeles.

A subsequent investigation uncovers the gritty truth: the "mummy" is, or was, train robber Elmer McCurdy (see October 7, 1911), whose body has been on quite a trip!

After he was killed by a posse in 1911, McGurdy's body lay unclaimed in an Oklahoma court house for four years until an alleged relative from California was given the corpse in 1916. From there, Elmer ended up in a travelling sideshow tent billed as "The Oklahoma Outlaw," and later, as "The Mummified Outlaw."

In 1925, a carnival barker used McGurdy as collateral on a $500 loan which he never repaid. At that time the outlaw was part of a travelling show of villains.

After several stints in storage, a fellow named Spoony Sing, bought Elmer in 1968 and put him in an exhibit called, "The 1,000 Year Old Man." Sing claimed it was his most popular exhibit.

After the Bad Man was discovered on The Pike, and it became news, historians from Oklahoma became bent on bringing him home.

ROY ROGERS · KING OF THE COWBOYS
starring in REPUBLIC'S MUSICAL WESTERNS

TWO GUN MEN

Roy Rogers (above) and Buck Jones (at left) show a similiar two gun stance (probably copied from William S. Hart). Although Roy played Billy the Kid in a movie he was anything but a Bad Man. Buck Jones sued the producers of the Lone Ranger for stealing his outfit (lace up front shirt, etc.) and his horse's name—Silver. Ouch! Jones made some 200 films. He died rescuing patrons from a Boston night club fire which took 500 lives in 1942. (AC)

THE DUKE OF BAD MEN

A big boy from Winterset, Iowa, Marion Michael Morrison played football at the University of Southern California (1925-27), and then got a job in Westerns as John Wayne. To the audiences of the late 20s and 30s he was masculine and refreshingly direct. His big break came in 1939 when he played a character loosely based on Johnny Ringo in *Stagecoach.* In his last movie, *The Shootist,* Wayne's character was loosely based on John Wesley Hardin. In it, the Duke was supposed to wear shoulder holsters as Hardin was alleged to have worn, but he looked too bulky with them on and the idea was scrapped. Having appeared in over 200 some odd movies, Wayne died of cancer at Westwood, California, in 1979. His reign as the number one action movie hero continues on into the millenium and shows no sign of diminishing. Ironically, he has become every bit as legendary as the Bad Men he portrayed. (AC)

April 23, 1977

Due to the efforts of Western author, Glenn Shirley, and various historical groups, 300 people attend the burial of outlaw Elmer McGurdy at the Boot Hill section of Summit View Cemetery in Stillwater, Oklahoma.

"We cannot condemn you because we don't know the conditions that existed in your time," Minister Glenn Jordon says. "We realize now that you were part of our heritage and a part of us and therefore with respect and decency we commit you to the earth."

January 24, 1999

Baseball great "Joltin' Joe" DiMaggio is watching his favorite movie, *Gunfight at the O.K. Corral,* while he recuperates from pneumonia and lung cancer surgery at his home in Hollywood, Florida. When Joe's neighbor and lawyer, Morris Engelberg shuts the tape off, they see a crawl report across the screen during *Dateline NBC* that claims DiMaggio has died.

"He was livid," Engelberg said. "Then I made him laugh. I said, 'Joe, we must be in heaven together.'"

[NBC delivered an apology to DiMaggio via Engelberg's office the next day. DiMaggio died on March 7, 1999.]

WHERE HAVE YOU GONE, DOC HOLLIDAY?

Kirk Douglas played Doc Holliday in Gunfight at the O.K. Corral, *1957. Other actors to play the good doctor include Victor Mature, Harry Carey, Cesar Romero, Walter Houston, Jason Robards, Adam West, Dennis Hopper, Stacey Keach, Val Kilmer and Dennis Quaid.* (AC)

ADIOS

• **Mickey Free,** the Apache captive, outlived two wives and most of his enemies. He died at the Fort Apache Reservation on New Year's Eve, 1913.

• **Frank James,** lived long enough to charge tourists a quarter each for a pebble off of Jesse's grave. He died peacefully, at the family farm on February 18, 1915.

• **Harry Morse,** lived until 1912, he died peacefully in bed and left a $100,000 estate to his heirs.

• **Bill Tilghman,** was still a lawman (although it should be noted he was hired by a company, he was not the official law) at age 70, when he was shot and killed, in 1924, while policing a rough oil boom town east of Oklahoma City. Bat Masterson described Tilghman as "the greatest of us all."

• **Cole Younger,** the sole survivor of the three outlaw Youngers, returned to his home at Lee's Summit, Missouri. He toured on and off, lecturing on "Crime Does Not Pay," or "What Life Has Taught Me," and once appeared with Frank James in a Wild West show. He died in 1916 with a purported 17 bullet wounds still in his body.

• **Bat Masterson,** became a celebrated sports writer in New York City, working for the *Morning Telegraph.* He attended fights, gambled and, so the story goes, was the inspiration for the character Sky Masterson in *Guys and Dolls.*

Bat died at his desk in 1921, after typing this paragraph: "There are many in this old world of ours who hold that things break about even for us. I have observed for example, that we all get about the same amount of ice.

A RESPECTABLE GROSS

Geronimo rode in Teddy Roosevelt's inauguration parade, and became a much in demand celebrity at fairs and events. He charged for his autograph and to sit for photographs. When he died in 1908 (with $10,000 in the bank!), he was still a prisoner of war, at Fort Sill, Oklahoma.
(EDWARD CURTIS PHOTOGRAPH)

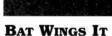

BAT WINGS IT

Bat Masterson had quite a career and he also inadvertantly, launched his friend's career. Masterson told a young writer, "the real story of the Old West can never be told unless Wyatt Earp will tell what he knows; and Wyat will not talk." Not long afterwards, Masterson died and the young writer, Stuart Lake, went west to find the aged lawman. His book "Frontier Marshal" sealed his fame.
(JEFF MOREY COLLECTION)

WYATT'S LAST PHOTO

The infamous gambler, miner and lawman in his last years, developed his mining interests near Parker, Arizona, and wanted to get his version of his life story out. He died in 1929 and didn't live to see Lake's book. (JEFF MOREY COLLECTION)

HONORARY PALL BEARERS AT WYATT EARP'S FUNERAL

It was an impressive group of friends who stood up for Wyatt at his funeral in Los Angeles. (left to right) W.J. Hunsaker (the Dean of the Los Angeles Bar), George Parsons, John Clum (both Tombstone friends), movie star William S. Hart, writer Wilson Mizner and famous cow-boy, Tom Mix. (LEE SILVA)

The rich get it in the summer time and the poor get it in the winter."

• **Tap Duncan,** bankrolled movies, prospered on his ranch and loved to ride good horse flesh, but unfortunately he was on foot when he was run over by a car just off Route 66 in Kingman, Arizona, in 1946.

• **Teddy Roosevelt,** the "Fearless Bugger" went on to glory on San Juan Hill, became president in 1901 with the death of McKinley. As "The Cow-boy President" Roosevelt set aside about 230 million acres of national forest lands, including more than 50 wildlife refuges and doubling the number of national parks. He died at Oyster Bay, Long Island, the family home, in 1919.

• **Commodore Perry Owens,** ended up in the saloon business at Seligman, Arizona, where he lived out his life in comparative peace and quiet. He died in 1919.

• **Gregorio Cortez,** returned to Texas, after fighting against Pancho Villa. He died suddenly after celebrating his fourth marriage. He was 41.

• **The Apache Kid,** simply disappeared. In 1899, Emil Kosterlisky, the head of the rurales in Sonora, Mexico, reported that the Apache Kid was living peacefully in the Sierra Madre with remnants of his people. How and when he actually died is not known.

• **Judge Roy Bean,** became a national character and when he died in 1903 the nation's press noted his passing. Ten months after his burial, Lily Langtry, the famous actress he had named his saloon after, came to Langtry, Texas, where she was presented with his pistol.

EMMETT DALTON
He was pardoned after serving 14 years in the penitentiary, then entered the real estate business in California, wrote a bestseller, "When the Daltons Rode" which was made into a movie. He died at age 65 in Los Angeles.
(BOB MCCUBBIN COLLECTION)

THE MAN WITH NINE LIVES
Elfego Baca loved to show off his two-gun style as shown here. Walt Disney created a TV show of his life in the 50s and Baca enjoyed his 15 minutes of fame. (MUSEUM OF NEW MEXICO)

• **Pancho Villa,** retired to his big house in Chihuahua, went for a drive in 1923 and was killed by a sharpshooter (probably sent by his former military rival, Alvaro Obregoon, who was president at the time).

• **Elza Lay,** of the Wild Bunch, was pardoned in 1906, allegedly dug up the loot (some say $50,000) from an 1899 train robbery, got remarried and lived out his life as a law abiding citizen (if you don't count the stolen money he spent). He had a drinking problem, but his wife stood by him. He died in 1934 and is buried at Forest Lawn Memorial Park cemetery in Glendale, California (the same cemetery Tom Mix is buried in).

• **Elfego Baca,** was admitted to the New Mexico bar in 1894, served as mayor, county clerk, school superintendent and district attorney and later was elected sheriff of Socorro County. Controversial to the end, he killed a Mexican assailant in El Paso during the Mexican Revolution and was acquitted. He lived through both world wars and died in 1945, at age 80.

• **Al Jennings,** bandit and lawyer (some claim that's redundant), ran for governor of Oklahoma (he came in a respectable third!). He made movies and toured the country as a speaker, although he suffered from Oldtimer's disease: every time he told a story he got closer to the center of the stage. By the 1950s he was telling disjointed windys about hobnobbing with Jesse James, Bat Masterson, Wyatt Earp and Doc Holliday. Well into his nineties, Jennings accidently shot and killed a 72-year-old friend while demonstrating his quick draw. He died peacefully at the ripe old age of 98, in 1961.

THE END OF THE INNOCENCE

Every year tens of thousands of tourists visit the American West to to get a taste of what it must have been like to have been alive a century ago. They avidly watch mock gunfights in Tombstone and Deadwood and cheer the horseback outlaws who pull a sham train robbery on the Grand Canyon Railway.

November 9, 1998

Tourists aboard a train on the Chihuahua-Pacific railway to Copper Canyon, Mexico, are robbed by 10-16 bandits who board the train as it enters a tunnel.

A Swiss tourist is shot and killed when he attempts to videotape the outlaws.

The terrorized passengers are held hostage for 30 to 40 minutes as the bandits go person to person, guns drawn, demanding money, gold and silver. "They just came down the aisle pointing guns at each one of our heads," one of the victims related. "[They were] shouting, 'Dolares! Dolares! No pesos! Dolares!"

After cleaning out the last car, the bandits disappear into the thick underbrush.

As the train begins moving, the wounded are cared for by passengers, some of whom are doctors. At least five suffered bullet wounds and one was pistol-whipped.

Understandably, tourist travel aboard the Copper Canyon train was down 80 percent in the months following the attack, but given what we now know about the Old West Bad Men, will there be a reenactment aboard this same train, a century from now? And will the descendents of the passengers on this train cheer for the outlaws? Bet on it.

DESPERADOES WAITING FOR A TRAIN

Three "outlaws" (above) attack the Williams to Grand Canyon, Arizona, train in 1991. Much to the delight of the tourist packed train, the Bad Men left their horses, climbed aboard and walked through the cars pointing their guns and threatening to rob the passengers. Everyone on board knew the drill and threw up their hands. "Don't shoot!" they said laughing. To many it was the highlight of the trip. (BBB)

EL VIEJO Y NUEVO

(BBB)

THE SCENE OF THE CRIME

A Chihuahua-Pacific train chugs along the foothills of the Sierra Madres (above) and pulls into the Divisidaro Station at Copper Canyon. It was on this stretch, that the spectacular train robbery took place. (BBB)

BANDITOS WAITING FOR A TRAIN

A dozen "outlaws" attacked the Chihuahua to Copper Canyon, Mexico train in 1998. Much to the horror of the tourist packed train, the Bad Men climbed aboard and walked through the cars pointing their guns and threatening to rob the passengers. Everyone on board knew the drill and threw up their hands. "Don't shoot!" they pleaded, praying for their lives. Many swore they would never travel in Mexico again. (BBB)

IT ENDS WITH ALL THE BAD MEN DEAD

(BBB)

JESSE JAMES AS AN ANGEL.

In the movies, the Bad Men must die at the end of the story. And, of course, they're all dead now: the good, the bad and the faithful horse. Time has rendered them all to dust and afterthought.

Any accurate, honest appraisal of their collective lives would have to be: they were *unworthy*.

"After all," my therapist wife might say, "they left nothing but sorrow in their wakes: good and bad families alike were shamed by their lethal dishonesty and any redeeming qualities they possessed were destroyed by their selfish and immature behavior (no wonder we men love them so much!)."

More criminal than cow-boy, less heroic than barbaric, the real Bad Men of the historic West were rightfully punished and when possible, destroyed. Yet, as film director Frances Ford Coppola succinctly puts it, "Everyone loves outlaws."

And, in spite of their unworthiness in life, they reign supreme in death (see pullquote at left).

Today we who are fascinated by them fight over footnotes and minutiae. What color were their hatbands and what was in their pockets when they fell? We have become nitpickers and whiners. It is doubtful that any of the real Bad Men would have a thing to do with us. I can picture Buckskin Frank Leslie reading this book and declaring: "Tell the author if I had some cartridges where I am, I'd do business with him." (AC)

"A man in his 20s, dressed in a sweatshirt and jeans, was scanning the tombstones in the Virginia City [Nevada] Cemetery. 'Where are the outlaws buried?' he asked as I walked by. I told him there were few or no outlaw graves. He walked away, got in his car, and drove off."

—CHUCK WOODBURY,
OUT WEST NEWSPAPER

CREDITS

Dedicated to my father, Allen P. Bell.
A good man by any measure.

Special Thanks to:

Bob McCubbin, for the use of his stellar collection of Bad Men photos (check out all the photo credits throughout the book and if Bob doesn't own the photo, it merely means he hasn't got around to buying it yet); the Movie Minutiae Man, **Jeff Morey,** who is always willing to share his passonate, yet professional opinions and research on the West and Western movies; **John Boessenecker**, who proofed my manuscript and added many entries and had numerous suggestions; **Dan Buck** (for also proofing the Butch material) and **Anne Meadows,** for their tireless and breakthrough research on Butch & Sundance in South America; **Jim Dullenty,** for his lifetime of research on Butch Cassidy (and for his phone seminar on the same subject before my trip to New York); prolific author, **Glenn Shirley,** for the use of his Henry Starr photos and for his personal tour of the Ingall's fight site and also the Bill Doolin death site; **Marcus Huff,** editor of *True West* magazine, for all his inspiration and help; **Phil Steward,** of the **Jesse James Farm**; **Lee Pollock,** for the use of his mighty fine Jesse collection; **Bill Secrest,** for his lifetime of research on California outlaws and for his "scrapbook" images; **Carl Chafin, Harold Roberts, Harry Jackson, Jim Jackson** of **Foothills Art Gallery, Marshall Trimble, Peggy Stewart, Gary McClellan,** for his C.S. Fly expertese; **Mike Clancy,** of the *Arizona Republic.* Special thanks to **Sheila Kollasch, Michael Ettema** and **Roxie Glover,** of the **Desert Caballeros Museum** in Wickenburg, who honored me with a one-man show featuring my art from this book. And thanks to **Craig Coffman, Phil Boag, Gretchen Kates, Aliza Trujillo** and **Meredith Depaolo** at **DVTV** who made me bone up on Butch Cassidy for their Gunfighter series on the **Learning Channel.** Thanks to **Howard Bryan,** for the Elfego Baca inside info; **Paul Northrop,** for always being ready to ride any trail, north or south of the border; **Nelson Wren, Jr.** for his expertise on the Wilcox train robbery; **Bob Steinhilber,** for his maps and lettering; **George Notarpole** of **History by George**; **Donna** and **Paul Ernst,** for the use of the "Tea Party" photo; **John Armstrong, Joan Prior** and printing assistant, **Michael Stevenson** of **Armstrong Prior Printmaking** of Phoenix for the wonderful chine colle! And last, but not least, **Pam Eckert** and her assistant, **Paul Sunbury** for the excellent framing.

Design and Computer Graphics:

Typography, layout, color, photo enhancement and electronic wizardry by **Tri Star Visual Communications,** Phoenix, Arizona, **Chris Sicurella,** and **Ted Kelley.** Edited by **Theresa Broniarczyk.**

Models:

Flint Carney, Dan Duffy, Lonnie Peters, Richard Ignarski, Matthias Ripken, Billy Lang.

Books & Authors I Stole From Shamelessly:

Henry Starr: Last of the Real Badmen, by **Glenn Shirley** (McKay); *Lawman: The Life and Times of Harry Morse,* by **John Boessenecker** (Oklahoma); *The Train Robbery Era,* by **Richard Patterson** (Pruett); *Encyclopedia of Western Gunfighters,* by **Bill O'Neal** (Oklahoma); *Encyclopedia of Frontier Biography,* by **Dan Thrapp** (Bison); *America West: A Historical Chronology,* by **Keith Cochran** (Cochran); *The War, the West and the Wilderness,* by **Kevin Brownlow,** (Knoph); *The Outlaw Youngers,* by **Marley Brant** (Madison); *Jesse James Was His Name,* by **William Settle, Jr**. (U of Missouri); *Guardian of the Law: The Life and Times of William Matthew Tilghman,* by **Glenn Shirley** (Eakin); *An Arizona Chronology: The Territory Years, 1846-1912,* by **Douglas Martin** (U of Arizona); *Digging Up Butch And Sundance,* by **Anne Meadows** (Saint Martins Press); *The Biographical Album of Western Gunfighters,* by **Ed Bartholomew** (Frontier Press); *Gold Dust & Gunsmoke,* by **John Boessenecker** (John Wiley, & Sons).

(BBB)